GRADES 5-9

The Seven C's of Thinking Clearly

Character Based Learning Activities
for Developing Emotional, Social, and Thinking Skills

BY GEORGE L. ROGERS

ILLUSTRATED BY GERALD ROGERS

SOUTH HUNTINGTON
PUBLIC LIBRARY
HUNTINGTON STATION, NY 11746

ChoiceSkills • P.O. Box 54 • Midvale, Utah

www.choiceskills.com

Publisher's Cataloging-in-Publication
(Provided by Quality Books, Inc.)

Rogers, George L., 1938-
   The seven C's of thinking clearly, grades 5-9 :
character based learning activities for developing
emotional, social, and thinking skills / by George L.
Rogers ; illustrated by Gerald Rogers. -- 1st ed.
   p. cm.
   Includes index
   LCCN 2001094623
   ISBN 0-938399-13-6

   1. Thought and thinking--Study and teaching (Middle
school)--United States. 2. Social skills--Study and
teaching (Middle school)--United States. 3. Education,
Elementary--Activity programs--United States.
I. Rogers Gerald, 1974- II. Title.

   LB1590.3.R64 2002   372.13
                                QBI98-500020

NOTE: Every effort has been made to identify the author and or copyright holder for every story and activity in this book. In those instances where it has not been possible to do so, I have noted the article as "Author Unknown." Should the reader happen to know the source of any of these stories, I will be happy to correct future editions.

Although only some selections are so noted, I am the author, though not necessarily the originator, of all other stories, biographical sketches, and activities in this book.

TABLE OF CONTENTS

INTRODUCTION

In 1728, Benjamin Franklin wrote an article for the *Weekly Mercury* in which he commented on what he thought the first priority of education ought to be.

"It is said that the Persians, in their constitution, had public schools in which virtue was taught as a liberal art or science; and it is certainly of more consequence to a man that he has learnt to govern his passions in spite of temptation, to be just in his dealings, to be temperate in his pleasures, to support himself with fortitude under his misfortunes, to behave with prudence in all his affairs and every circumstance of life; I say, it is of much more real advantage to him to be thus qualified, than to be master of all the arts and sciences in the world besides."

Benjamin Franklin's The Art of Virtue, p. 21

But, how do you teach children to govern their passions and to be good neighbors and citizens? How do you teach them to be just in their dealings, temperate in their pleasures, and to behave with prudence? How do you teach them these qualities without constantly lecturing, nagging, scolding and punishing them?

The first answer, of course, is in modeling these qualities ourselves so they can see what they look like.

The second answer is to provide them with character based learning experiences wherein they come to understand the immense value of these qualities for themselves.

Character based learning is learning in which students are:

1) Acquiring useful knowledge
2) Developing their thinking skills, and
3) Strengthening their character

all at the same time, or as part of the same learning experience.

The acquisition of knowledge, is the first business of youth. And, though most young people don't realize it, the knowledge they acquire in this season of their lives is the foundation on which they must build for the future. This is not only important for them personally, it is also critical to the future of the societies in which they live. Gaining a solid understanding of the arts and sciences is not merely an amusing pastime, it is serious business and begins at an early age. Individuals and nations who are unsuccessful in this endeavor are severely disadvantaged.

The strengthening of one's character is no less an essential ingredient in one's education. Mutual respect for one another is a primal ingredient for a happy and productive life and an essential glue in holding communities and nations together. But mutual respect can only exist where there is mutual trust and where individuals take personal responsibility for their choices and actions.

The development of thinking skills is fundamental to both the acquisition of knowledge and the strengthening of one's character. Neither can fully occur without well developed thinking skills.

Here we are not talking about intellectual capacity. It is possible to be very bright without being very wise. We're talking about the kind of thinking skills Benjamin Franklin was referring to when he wrote:

". . .as the happiness or real good of men consists in right action, and right action cannot be produced without right opinion, it behooves us, above all things in this world, to take care that our own opinions of things be according to the nature of things. The foundation of all virtue and happiness is thinking rightly."

Ibid. p 29

In fact, the seven C skills in *The Seven C's of Thinking Clearly* are specific skills Franklin consciously developed in his own life to help him avoid the problems of faulty thinking. Although Franklin was one of the brightest men to have ever lived, he didn't trust human reason, "...since it enables one to find or make a reason for everything one has a mind to do."

Character based learning can be experienced while learning how to read or write, how to add or subtract, how to play a game, or how to put away one's clothes. Character based learning can be experienced while learning about health, science, history, music, woodworking or any of the myriad things we are constantly teaching children to do.

Since, thinking skills are essential both the acquisition of knowledge and character development, the first two sections *Seven C's of Thinking* are focused on thinking skills.

In Section One students are introduced to EPT, a clandestine organization whose mission is to flood the world with Error-Prone thinking. Since faulty thinking lies at the root self-defeating behavior, students need to learn how to recognize and overcome this common enemy.

The EPT characters are not actually part of any of the stories or activities, but rather are used as a discussion device to explore faulty thinking practices in fun, objective, and non-threatening ways.

In Section Two students learn about the seven C skills—Criticism, Creativity, Communication, Concentration, Curiosity, Correction, and Control—and why they need to develop these skills.

Sections Four through Six are focused respectively on helping students develop Personal Responsibility, Self-Respect, Respect for Others and Trustworthiness.

Notwithstanding the focus of each section, every lesson in *The Seven C's of Thinking Clearly* is multidimensional and may be presented from more than one point of view.

- Each lesson has a learning component such as reading, writing, social studies, math, science, art, music, etc.
- Every lesson has a character development component and provides an opportunity to explore one or more specific character traits.
- Finally, there is a thinking skills component in every lesson that provides students opportunities to examine and develop one or more thinking skills.

To simplify preparation, lessons are accompanied with a discussion opportunity box and/or hindsight, insight, and foresight questions.

Hindsight, Insight, and Foresight questions provide practical exercises in critical thinking.

Hindsight Questions are used to help young people learn from experience—their own experience and the experiences of others. All too many youth go through life as if no one has ever lived before, repeating mistakes of the past.

Insight Questions are used to help young people understand why things are the way they are and how they got that way—in other words, to understand the nature of things.

Foresight Questions are used to help young people learn how to anticipate the probable or likely consequences of their choices.

If we can help young people develop the discipline of looking back at the past to see what has happened, to look at the nature of what it is they are contemplating doing, and to anticipate the possible outcomes, they will be in a much stronger position to make responsible choices.

Most lessons may be prepared in a matter of minutes and presented in a variety of ways. For example, a given lesson may be presented in a 20-minute block, two 10-minute blocks, or four 5-minute blocks and the discussion may focus on thinking skills on one occasion and character development on another. .

Where advance preparation is required, the requirements are noted by the words ADVANCE PREPARATION with a description of the preparation required.

An Index to the rich literature base contained in this book may be found on pages 165 and 167 under the headings "Great Lessons From Great Lives" and "Great Lessons From Great Literature." You will find these stories, not only entertaining, but also inspiring reading. They will provide you many ideas on how you might want to approach the lessons contained herein.

CHOOSING TO AVOID ERROR-PRONE THINKING

Section One

LEARNING OBJECTIVES FOR SECTION ONE

The ability to recognize different forms of error-prone thinking

A basic understanding of the difficulties caused by error-prone thinking

It leads people to want things that aren't good for them

It leads people to not want things that are good for them

It leads people to overvalue or undervalue the importance of things

It leads people to be dishonest with each other

It leads people to form opinions contrary to the nature of things

A desire to develop safe guards against them

SECTION OVERVIEW

Benjamin Franklin once wrote, ". . . .as the happiness or real good of men consists in right action and right action cannot be produced without right opinion, it behooves us, above all things in this world to take care that our own opinions of things be according to the nature of things. The foundation of all virtue and happiness is thinking rightly." (*Benjamin Franklin's the Art of Virtue*, pp. 29, 30)

Unfortunately, there are several common, even prevalent, thinking habits which are highly error-prone and severely inhibit our ability to think rightly. They are error-prone because they alter, distort, or ignore information necessary to forming a correct understanding of the nature of things. People who indulge in them are vulnerable to making choices that complicate and sometimes ruin their lives. In this book we focus on eight habits of error-prone thinking. They are presented as the E's and P's of EPT, secret agents engaged in an insidious plan to contaminate the world with error-prone thinking. They are led by the sinister twin sisters Erroneous and Emotious.

Erroneous is a cunning psychologist who plays games with the mind. She is aided by two well placed, highly skilled agents known as Prevaricator and Perverter.

Prevaricator's job is to get people to believe things that aren't true. He attempts to convince people to lie and deliberately mislead others. He is so skillful he can frequently even get people to lie to themselves. Perverter blows things out of proportion so people lose perspective. He does this by befogging their thinking. Puff Belarge and things seem more important, more urgent, more valuable, and more desirable or more frightening than they really are. Puff Belittle and things seem less important, less significant, and less valuable than they really are. With a Puff Prejudge befogger, the victim believes he already knows everything that needs to be known about any given person, idea or thing. With a Puff Benamed Puff Beblamed befogger, Perverter can get people to assign estimates of worth to an individual or class of people with a single word or phrase.

Emotious excels at agitating emotions in unsuspecting victims. She works with three equally effective secret agents who go by the code names of Possessit., Passionata and Polarizer.

Possessit tries to infect people with the "I Want Bias." When so infected, people are willing to believe any argument that favors their wants and are equally unwilling to consider to any argument that runs contrary to their wants. Passionata is the one who is responsible for firing up a person's emotions to the point where the victim is being completely controlled by unrestrained passion. In this condition, rational thought and responsible choices are no longer possible. When Possessit and Passionata are in control; hate, envy, lust, greed and other raw feelings rule a person's choices. Polarizer feeds on these emotions. His job is to make people think they are enemies and put them at odds with each other. He also wants them to think things are polar opposites, either one way or the other—for example either good or bad, right or wrong, friend or enemy.

ACTIVITY 1

BEWARE OF ERROR-PRONE THINKING

1-1   EPT Intelligence Briefing

ADVANCE PREPARATION: *Prepare a copy of the Intelligence Briefing Scripts on pages 6–7. Assign four students to read specific parts and have them practice their parts in advance of class. Prepare overhead transparencies of pages 8 and 9 or use the EPT poster. Have readers 2 and 3 point to each character when reading about them. After the briefing refer to the HIF questions on page 5.*

Begin by telling the class:

You are members of an elite counterintelligence unit that has been created to detect and neutralize enemy agents from EPT. These agents are engaged in a massive disinformation plot designed to overthrow civilization. They have infiltrated our intelligence system and are causing great damage, both to individuals and to our society. You have been called to this emergency briefing to alert you to their activity and to give you an overview of who they are and how they operate. You will then begin a skill development process designed to help you identify and root out these menaces to our way of life.

This briefing will be under the direction of four crack members of your unit, (name script readers). Be sure to take notes on what you are told here. In the next few days, you will be tested on what you remember from today's briefing. This is for your own protection. I will now turn the briefing over to (name of Reader 1). *Reader 1 begins reading from the script provided.*

1-2   EPT Quiz

ADVANCE PREPARATION: *Prepare copies of pages 10 and 11 for each student.*
Have your students use the notes they made during the EPT intelligence briefing to complete the quiz. Discuss the HIF questions on page 5.

1-3   Observation Reports

Assign your students to select one or two EPT agents. Have them make notes on any instances they can observe of the influence of these agents in choices people make. The instances may be observed in movies, TV programs, music, news reports, or in real life situations (avoid mentioning names if the incident is close to home.) Then have them report to the rest of the class some of the instances they observed. Discuss the HIF questions on page 5.

1-4   Which EPT Agent is Poor Richard Talking About?

In 1732, Benjamin Franklin first published Poor Richard's Almanac. To help make the Almanac both interesting and useful, he filled all the little spaces that occurred between the days in the calendar with proverbial sentences. Following are several those proverbs. Read a proverb to your students and see if they can identify which form of error-prone thinking is represented in the proverb.

Vice knows she is ugly so she puts on her mask. (1746)

A man in a passion rides a mad horse. (1757)

It is easier to suppress the first desire than to satisfy all that follows it. (1757)

Man's tongue is soft, and bone doth lack;
Yet a stroke therewith may break a man's back. (1740)

Quarrels could never last long, If on one side only lay the wrong. (1741)

We are not so sensible of the greatest health as we are the least sickness. (1747)

A mob's a monster; Has heads enough but no brains. (1747)

Hindsight Questions
- What does EPT stand for?
- How are Erroneous and Emotious different?

Insight Questions
- How can prevaricating or falsifying information cause error-prone thinking?
- How can error-prone thinking lead a person to prevaricate or falsify information?
- How can perverting information by exaggerating or minimizing lead to poor choices?
- Why is a person with uncontrolled passions subject to error-prone thinking?
- How do strong wants or desires to possess something influence a person's thinking?

Foresight Questions
- Why is it important to recognize these various forms of error-prone thinking?

Discussion Opportunity: Error-prone thinking is thinking that is likely to lead to false or erroneous conclusions which, in turn, lead to poor choices. As Benjamin Franklin wrote, right actions are dependent on right opinions or opinions that are in agreement with the nature of things. In order to form right opinions, we need to be able to think clearly and to avoid all forms of error-prone thinking. Error-prone thinking may also originate from our emotions. If our emotions are stirred up, it is very difficult to think clearly. The ability to think clearly involves managing both mind and feelings, it involves both the head and the heart. Character Traits: All

Intelligence Briefing Scripts

Reader 1

As elite members of our counter-intelligence team, you have been called together this (morning/afternoon) to receive an emergency briefing on EPT. Its agents have infiltrated our intelligence operations and are causing immeasurable damage to our security system. I need not remind you these agents are well trained, highly effective, and very dangerous. The damage they cause runs into the billions of dollars every year and the destruction of thousands of lives. They are not to be taken lightly. If you encounter them, I should say, when you encounter them, for encounter them you will, it will require all your talents and skill to overcome them. They are clever. They are treacherous. And, they have no mercy. They will challenge your judgment. They will push you to the limits of your understanding. They will test your will and your determination to overcome their influence. The more of you they can recruit to their side, the greater their success. Unless you are fully prepared, mentally, physically, and emotionally, you will be in grave danger. I am going to turn the briefing over to (names of Reader 2 and Reader 3) from operations to give you a rundown on each of the EPT agents we are up against. After they are through, (Reader 4) will outline some of the training we will be providing to help you in dealing with these agents. You will need all the preparation you can get.

Reader 2

Here's what we have. I suggest you take notes. (Pause) Agents of EPT (Error-Prone Thinking) are engaged in an insidious plan to overthrow civilization. They intend to do this by contaminating the world with error-prone thinking. They have had great success in infiltrating our intelligence community of which you are an important part. I cannot overstate the risk you are facing. They will do anything they can to confuse your thinking. If they succeed, you will have great difficulty in making sound choices. Their goal is to ruin the lives of as many people as they can. So, who are we up against? The E's and P's of EPT are are led by the diabolical twin sisters, Erroneous and Emotious.

Erroneous is a master psychologist. She and the agents who work with her are highly skilled in the art of illusion. They want you to focus on the appearance and not the substance of things. They have the ability to change the appearance of almost anything. They can make you believe up is down, forward is back, and in is out. It's all in the mind you see, and if they can manipulate your thinking, they can get you to believe anything they want. Erroneous is aided by two well placed, highly skilled agents who are solidly entrenched in our intelligence system. In fact, they are so well established we hardly recognize their existence. We only know them by their code names, Prevaricator and Perverter.

Prevaricator is a master of deceit. His specialty is lying. Blatant lies, subtle lies, big lies, little lies. He has succeeded in making lying a common practice in our culture. From high government officials, to business leaders, to superstars, to out right crooks, to small children on the play ground, Prevaricator has persuaded many that deceit is the best way to get what they want or feel they need.

Perverter is a genius at blowing things out of proportion so people lose perspective. He is what is known as a Befogger. He functions by blowing smoke in people's eyes so things look differently to them than they really are. For example, if he blows:

Puff Belarge, you are enveloped in a cloud of smoke that makes things appear to be of greater value or importance, more urgent or serious of than they really are. When under the spell of Puff Belarge, you must have it, get it, do it now; whatever the cost in time, money, energy, talent, relationships, health, future well-being or whatever medium of exchange nature requires.

Puff Belittle, blows Perverter, and you are encased in a cloud of smoke that minimizes and belittles the value or importance of things in your mind. When under the influence of this befogger, you no longer recognize the true value or importance of things. It causes you to undervalue such things as cleaning your rooms, doing your home work, obeying rules, being honest, treating others kindly, etc. It causes you to minimize the seriousness and ignore the consequences of choices you make.

Puff Benamed Puff Beblamed befoggs you into thinking that a word or a phrase is capable of describing a whole class of people or ideas. The belief is, if you know the label you understand the person or idea. Many people fall for this myth because its easy. It requires little thought and instantly makes one an expert. Besides, when people can be named, they can be blamed for whatever the people who named them want to blame them. That's the neat trick of this befogger.

Puff Prejudge is another befogger that severely cripples the thinking of many people. The Puff Prejudge befogger convinces people that they know the worth of a person or idea without ever really knowing the person or understanding the idea. Moreover, based on these judgments, they are entitled to discriminate against and even persecute those people they judge to be of lesser worth than themselves or who hold ideas contrary to their own. This befogger enables people to justify such acts as slavery and the holocaust of WWII.

Reader 3

Emotious is expert in manipulating your emotions. Encouraging feelings of hate, anger, revenge, jealousy, fear, hopelessness, despair, greed, lust, and pride are some of her more common tactics. Such feelings, when strong enough, can block out all ability to think clearly. She works in close harmony with Erroneous, and together they can completely eliminate a person's ability to think and act responsibly. Emotious has three able and highly dangerous agents who work closely with her, Possessit, Passionata, and Polarizer.

Possessit is perhaps the most dangerous of all the E's and P's. He usually the first to infiltrate a person. He infects people with a desire to possess things. The more the better. If it is more than others, even better. Possession becomes a symbol of status and superiority over others. The desire to possess something can become so great an obsession that people will do or say anything to get what they want, no matter how potentially dangerous it is to themselves or to others.

Passionata is also known as the inflamer. Passionata takes natural desires and turns them into burning passions. Anger becomes rage. Attraction becomes lust. Appetite becomes greed. Dislike becomes hate. Discouragement becomes despair. Fear becomes cowardice. Normal feelings become uncontrollable emotions under whose influence disastrous deeds are done.

Polarizer divides people into two opposite camps. Under his influence, ideas are divided into two opposite views and choices are limited to two polar options. Polarizer is extremely effective in stirring up conflict and contention between individuals, families, communities, ethnic groups, and nations.

Reader 4

I know you're tired of sitting here and you're ready for action, so listen up. Because of the serious nature of the EPT threat, you will be required to take some specialized training. It will consist of exercises designed to acquaint you with the techniques and practices of EPT. That will be followed by training in the Seven C's of Thinking Clearly. This training will provide you with additional skills and tools in resisting the EPT's. The next stage of training will have to do with specific situations in which you will likely engage the EPT's and will require you to use your thinking skills in overcoming them. You will receive regular notices informing you of these training sessions. Ok, that's it for now.

ERRONEOUS

PREVARICATOR

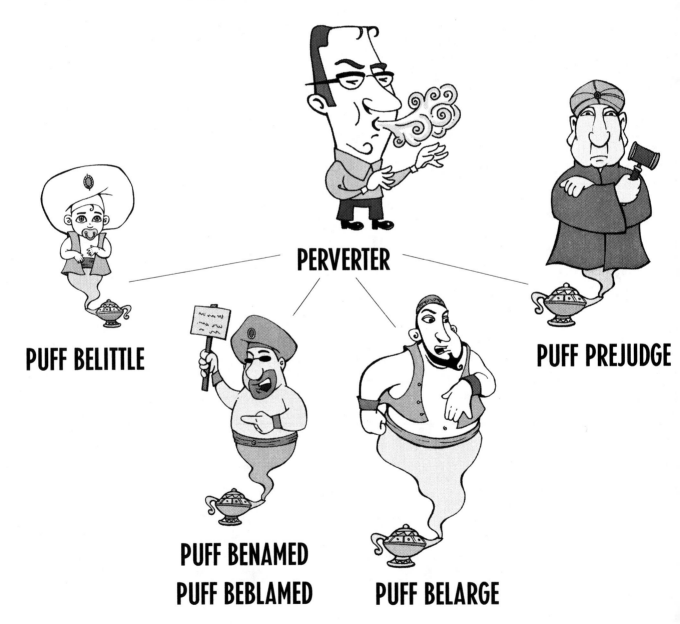

PERVERTER

PUFF BELITTLE

PUFF PREJUDGE

PUFF BENAMED
PUFF BEBLAMED

PUFF BELARGE

EMOTIOUS

POSSESSIT

PASSIONATA

POLARIZER

EPT QUIZ

Identify each agent of EPT by writing his or her name by the appropriate description

_____is a sinister psychologist who likes to play games with with your mind. She is sophisticated; she is clever; and she is merciless. She is a master in deception and illusion. To examine her handiwork is to witness the horrors of human folly.

Whether it is a family quarrel or a war between nations, she supplies the reasons. She provides the reasons that justify pornography, violent movies and TV programs. She can help a murder justify the act and a thief believe he is only getting what is due him. She is a wicked lady indeed.

_____is a master of deceit. His specialty is lying. He has succeeded in making lying a common practice among nearly all ages and stations in life. Perhaps his greatest success is in the area of self-deceit. Since no one will readily admit to being a liar, not even to themselves, to tell a lie, a person must first believe a lie. The lie may be, "I'll be better off if no one knows", or "It's their fault.", or perhaps, "It won't hurt anyone." But, there must always be a good reason for the lie, for who wants to be known as a liar?

_____is a specialist in illusions. He is what is known as a Befogger. He blows smoke in people's eyes so they have trouble seeing things in their true light.

He can make the important seem trivial and the trivial seem important. He can make friends appear to be enemies and enemies appear to be friends. He can make foolishness fashionable and common sense unpopular. He can make people believe being thin is more important than being healthy, being cool is more important than being kind, and being pretty is more important than being good. Under his influence, it's the appearance, not the substance that counts. The befoggers he uses are:

_____

to exaggerate and overvalue things

_____

to minimize or undervalue things

_____

to label people and things

_____

to create the illusion of knowledge where ignorance really exists _____is every bit as clever, cunning, and dangerous as her sister. Perhaps more so because she, and the agents she works with are capable, not only of playing games with the mind, but of blocking out all rational thought. Such are the power of the emotions.

She and her agents are principle players in most violent crimes. They have had particular success in recent years in dramatically increasing domestic violence. Her hand is in the terrible atrocities associated with "ethnic cleansing."

From armed conflict between nations to quarrels between friends, Emotious and her agents Possessit, Passionata and Polarizer, have been highly successful in ruining human lives.

_____is perhaps the most influential of all the EPT agents. It is he that creates the longings and desires that make it possible for Prevaricator, Perverter, Passionata, and Polarizer to get such strong holds on people. It all begins with their wants. If Possessit can make a person want something enough, the other agents can take those wants and work on them in ways that completely destroy the person's ability to think clearly and act rationally.

Under his influence, husbands abandon wives and children, children disobey parents, successful lawyers embezzle client funds, trusted employees sell company secrets, and teenagers worship popular icons who live ruinous lives. This is one influential guy. If he can make you want it bad enough, you will lose all sense of perspective and all ability to make good choices.

_____is the inflamer, the torch. She operates with a scorched earth policy. She leaves destruction in her wake and tallies her success in broken bodies, burned villages, and destroyed lives. Under her influence, a small flame can become a raging forest fire burning all in its path. She is present at nearly every murder, in every gang fight, and every battle in war. She is the principle instigator of domestic violence, road rage, airline rage, school rage, or any other rage you can imagine.

But her repertoire is greater than uncontrolled anger. She can turn love into obsession, fear into terror, and discouragement into despair. All of which are highly effective in leading people to make incredibly poor choices.

_____strategy is to divide and conquer. if he can get people to dislike each other he can get them to destroy each other. All he has to do is make them think they are on opposites sides of something. It doesn't matter much what. It could be the opposite side of town. It could be different religions or different colors of skin. Political views are particularly effective for him. When he's not persuading people they are enemies, he's convincing them their choices are limited to only two options or their problems only have two solutions. With him, things are always either or, there are no other options.

ACTIVITY 2

BRAIN FOOD FOR ERROR-PRONE THINKING

2-1 — Soap Flavored Cracker

Place some crackers in a closed container with soap flakes. Leave over night. Invite students to smell and taste the crackers. Which had the greater influence, the crackers or the soap?

2-2 — Mental Images

Draw a brain on the board and ask your students what kinds of brain foods may be harmful to their ability to think clearly. Explain that brain food is the information, ideas, pictures, and images we put into our minds. List their suggestions on the board. Ask: How do these kinds of mental food influence our thinking? What kinds of error-prone thinking do they encourage? How might this be hurtful to us? How do we feed our minds harmful mental food? How can we quit feeding our minds these hurtful ideas? What kind of mental food would be more beneficial to us? Where can we get good mental food?

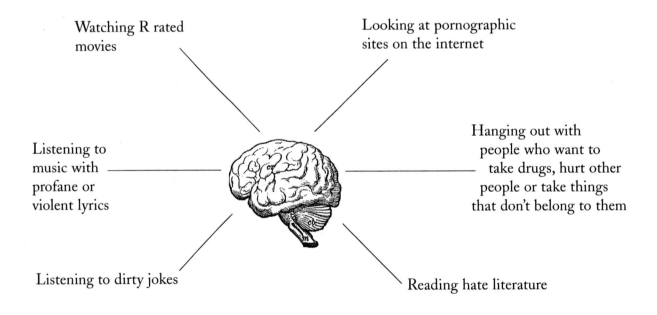

Watching R rated movies

Looking at pornographic sites on the internet

Listening to music with profane or violent lyrics

Hanging out with people who want to take drugs, hurt other people or take things that don't belong to them

Listening to dirty jokes

Reading hate literature

Discussion Opportunity: To avoid being influenced by Error-Prone Thinking, you have to avoid being in places where they hang out. If you expose yourself to people that encourage you to lie, like the cracker you will pick up the habit. If you frequently expose your mind to movies, music, or magazines that encourage you to think about sex or violence, you will pick up the habit. Your mind is very impressionable and will pick up the knowledge, the thinking habits, the ideas you choose to feed it. Character Traits: PR ownership; SR self-denial

ACTIVITY 3

SELF-TALK

ADVANCE PREPARATION: *Invite a student to help you record the following script onto an audio tape.*

Teacher: In class we have been learning about thinking. . . .

Student: I think Mom was sure grouchy this morning. Why she won't let me go to Ruthie's after school? I never get to do what I want. So what if my room is messy, I like it that way.

Teacher: . . .life be like if you did not have the ability to think?

Student: That must be my problem, I think too much. I'd like to live with Ruthie's parents. They let her do whatever she wants and they don't nag her all the time about her room.

Teacher: Some of that happens naturally when you grow older.

Student: Huh? What happens naturally? What did I miss?

Teacher: . . . .more control over your thinking than you had when you were younger.

Student: Control my thinking? My mind goes in a hundred directions. Hum, I really like Sandy's sweater. It's really pretty. I want one like it. I wonder if Mom would get me one.

Begin the activity by reading the following:

In class we have been learning about thinking. Can you imagine what life would be like if you did not have the ability to think? What could you do? What could you become? How does the ability to think make people different than animals such as dogs or cats or elephants or monkeys? But just like any other skill, the ability to think needs to be developed and improved. Some of that happens naturally as you grow older. Just as you have gained more control over your body as you have grown older, you have also gained more control over your thinking than you had when you were younger. In the same way it is possible to train your bodies to do specific things such as running and jumping or to play a piano, it is possible to train your mind to think more clearly in learning new things and in solving problems.

Explain that while you have been talking to them, they have also been talking to themselves. Play the tape recording as an example of self-talk. Being aware of our self-talk helps us be aware of our thinking.

- What was the teacher talking about?
- What was the student thinking and talking about?
- How much do you think the student heard?

Discussion Opportunity: During our waking hours, our minds are always running. A good part of that time we are talking to ourselves. What we say to ourselves is very important. When we let our minds just run, they will take the course of least resistance and focus on things of greatest interest or closest proximity. This is one reason we need to be very careful of what we feed our minds and how we take care of them. By learning to detect error-prone thinking in others, and then by paying attention to what we say to ourselves, we can recognize error-prone thinking within ourselves and will be in a better position to correct it. Character Traits: PR ownership; SR self-reliance

ACTIVITY 4

TV WATCH

4-1 _____ Advertising's Best Friends

George Will wrote an article "Born to be Consumers" published in the May 6, 2001 edition of *The New York Times*. In the article, he talks about advertisers who target child consumers and the sophisticated behavioral studies they use to manipulate young people's attitudes. In the article, Will quoted one advertiser as saying, "Advertising at its best is making people feel that without their product you're a loser. Kids are very sensitive to that."

Assign students to watch advertising on TV and take notes on ways in which advertisers try to get people, and especially young people, hooked on their products. Provide the following questions as clues for things they should take notes on. 1) How might Possessit, Perverter, and Prevaricator be considered advertising's best friends? 2) What is the advertiser trying to get people to do? 3) What illusions does the advertiser create to make people want their product? 4) In what ways, if any, did the advertiser try to create the illusion that people who use their product are winners, and those who don't are losers? 5) In what ways might the advertisement may be stretching or even altering the truth? Give extra credit to students who video tape advertisements they think really demonstrate the influence of EPT.

4-2 _____ Really Watching TV

Assign students to identify and make notes on the influence of Possessit, Perverter, Prevaricator, and Passionata on various characters in TV programs they watch. 1) What did the character want? 2) How did the character exaggerate or minimize the importance or value of people and things? 3) If people were in conflict, what was it that polarized them? 4) To what extent were labels or names attached to different groups or ideas? 5) Did prejudice have any influence on the characters? 6) To what extent did the characters engage in deceit? 7) How much influence did their emotions and passions have on their choices? Again, give extra credit for especially instructive video clips illustrating these influences.

Hindsight Questions
• How difficult was it to find examples of error-prone thinking in advertising/TV programs?

Insight Questions
• How do you feel about the use of these techniques by advertisers?
• How do advertisers justify the use of these techniques?
• Why are Possessit, Perverter, and Prevaricator Advertiser's best friends?
• What can you learn about error-prone thinking by watching TV and movies?

Foresight Questions
• Why is it important to recognize error-prone thinking when you see encounter it?
• Why is it important to be aware of their use by advertisers?

ACTIVITY 5

EPT AGENTS AT WORK

Pages 16 and 17 provide the basis for the following five activities. They contain examples of error-prone thoughts and potential problems that may be created by that form of thinking. They are grouped by type of error-prone thought. These ways of thinking are error-prone because they lead us to believe things that are not correct and often cause us to act in ways that are hurtful to ourselves and others.

5-1 ADVANCE PREPARATION: *Photocopy the activity sheets on pages 16-17. Have your students match each error-prone thought with the problem they think will result from that way of thinking by drawing a line from each thought to the associated problem.*

5-2 *Select statements from the EPT's on pages 16 and 17 to read to your students. After each statement have them tell you which EPT is influencing that thought and give an example of situations in which someone might say something like that.*

5-3 *Assign your students to write a short story in which the characters in the story are influenced by two or more forms of EPT in choices they make in the story.*

5-4 *Have students keep a log for two or three days of their own EPT thoughts and then provide a written or verbal report on their experience. For example, how many times did they mentally label a person or idea, or how often did they blame someone else for something that happened to them? Did they lose their temper, really want something, or engage in either/or or polarized thinking? How many times did they they exaggerate or minimize something? Have them identify, as best as they can, why they felt a need or were inclined to use these EPT patterns.*

Hindsight Questions
- What does error-prone mean?
- What makes a thinking pattern error-prone?

Insight Questions
- How do error-prone thinking habits influence our choices?
- How may error-prone thinking habits create difficulties for us?

Foresight Questions
- Why is it important to be able to recognize error-prone thinking?

Discussion Opportunity: If we are observant, we can recognize error-prone thinking all around us and even within ourselves. Error-prone thinking represents a risk to us, both when used by others and especially when used by ourselves. Error-prone thinking tends to produce errors in understanding and judgment which, in turn, lead to faulty choices. Character Traits: PR ownership

---

ERROR-PRONE THINKING MATCHING ACTIVITY

Draw a line from each error-prone thought (EPT) to the problem associated with that way of thinking.

Prevaricator, Falsifying, Lying

Prevaricating is deliberately using false information to mislead others. It includes leaving out, changing, and outright fabrication of information designed to make people believe things that aren't true.

EPT	Problem With
"If someone asks, I'll say I found it."	May find out wasn't there, loss of trust
"I'll tell her I was at Marvin's."	Fear of discovery by owner, always on guard

Perverter, Distorting, Warping, Twisting

Perverter blows smoke in people's eyes to make things appear better or worse than they really are. He uses the following befoggers to lead people to make poor choices.

Puff Belarge, Magnifying, Exaggerating

The Puff Belarge befogger makes things seem more important, more valuable, more beneficial, more scary, more difficult, more unpleasant than they really are. It causes people to have unreasonable wants and fears leading them to do foolish things.

EPT	Problem With
"I want that bike more than anything."	Unreasonable fear, lack of effort
"They're so good. We don't stand a chance."	Willing to pay more than it's worth

Puff Belittle, Minimizing or Understating

The Puff Belittle befogger makes things seem less important, less valuable, less dangerous, less serious, than they really are. It causes people to be underestimate the worth of things leading them to be careless, indifferent and to lack appropriate concern for making responsible choices.

EPT	Problem With
"School's just not important to me."	Under estimate seriousness
"Just once can't hurt."	Not enough effort to succeed

Puff Benamed Puff Beblamed

The Puff Benamed befogger convinces people to using single words and phrases to express complete thoughts. It causes people to love or hate other people and things they really know little about. Labeling is a frequently way of trying to build one's self up by tearing someone else down.

EPT	Problem With
"He's a loser."	Prejudice people's thinking for or against
"One's pro-life, the other's pro-choice."	Discounts worth, inability to see potential

Puff Prejudge, Prejudice or Bias

The Puff Prejudge befogger causes people to prejudge things before getting full and accurate information. Prejudice is highly error-prone because partial and inaccurate information seldom leads to sound conclusions.

EPT	Problem With
"People are poor because they're lazy."	Treat others disrespectfully
"Your kind doesn't belong here."	Failure to recognize real problem

Polarizer

Polarizer leads people to believe that only two options exist which are generally the extreme opposites of each other. Such polarized thinking often puts people in adversarial positions and limits their ability to find creative solutions to problems.

EPT	Problem With
"Either your for or against me."	Discourages cooperation
"Either you do it my way or not at all."	Creates conflict

Possessit

Possessit creates the "I Want" bias in people, causing them to want things that aren' t good for them and not want things that are good for them. The greater the desire, the greater the bias. This bias leads people to accept arguments in favor of what they want and disregard arguments contrary to what they want.

EPT	Problem With
"I don't want to take my medicine"	May not get well
"I want to be popular."	Dependence on external recognition of worth

Passionata

Passionata inflames emotions to the point people do not think and act clearly. When emotions are in control, people often do and say things they later regret.

EPT	Problem With
"I hate her."	Keeps from trying, limits growth
"I won't go out there. I'm afraid."	Creates unhappiness, disrespect, contention

ACTIVITY 6

WHAT DOES IT COST?

Have your students solve the following math problems. Each problem involves three pieces of information: 1) the price of an item, 2) the dollars per hour a person earns, and 3) the number of hours the person must work in order to purchase that item. In each of the following problems two of the three pieces of information are given. They are to solve for the third.

Question 1
Emily baby sits for several people. She gets $3.00 per hour. Emily wants to buy a new pair of roller blades that cost $42.00. How many hours will she have to baby sit to buy the roller blades she wants? $42/$3/hr. = 14 hrs.

Question 2
Charles just bought a new bicycle for $125. Charles figured he had to work 20 hours to earn enough money to buy his bike. How much money does Charles earn per hour? $125/20hrs. = $6.25/hr.

Question 3
Rosalie works in a grocery store on weekends and evenings for $5.00 per hour. She wants to get a CD for her brother for his birthday. She figured it would take her 2 1/2 hours to earn enough money to buy the CD and pay the sales tax. How much money will it cost Rosalie to get the CD? 2.5 hrs. X $5/hr. = $12.50

Hindsight Questions
- What did these people spend to buy money?

Insight Questions
- How are time, effort, and money measures of what we want?
- What is a good indication of how much we want something?
- What is a hidden cost each of these people might want to think about?

Foresight Questions
- Why is it important to give thought as to how you spend your time?
- Why may it be beneficial for you to invest in developing your talents?

Discussion Opportunity: How much we are willing to spend, in time, energy, money, or other resources to get something is a direct measure of how much we want something. When we exchange time for money we are saying the money is more important to us than the time. When we spend money to buy something, we are saying the thing is more important to us than the money. A hidden cost is that when we spend our time for one thing it is not available for something else. The same is true with money. Since most of us have limited time, money, and other resources we need to be careful in how we spend them. Character Traits: PR duty; SR self-reliance

---

ACTIVITY 7

DON'T PAY TOO MUCH FOR THE WHISTLE

Adapted from the writings of Benjamin Franklin

In my opinion we might all draw more good from this world than we do, and suffer less evil, if we would take care not to give too much for our whistles. For to me it seems that most unhappy people have become so by neglect of that caution.

You ask what I mean? You love stories, and will excuse my telling one of myself.

When I was a child of seven years old, some friends visiting on a holiday filled my pocket with coppers. I went directly to a shop where they sold toys for children, but along the way I met with a boy who was blowing on a whistle that charmed me very much. I voluntarily offered and gave him all of my money for his whistle. I then came home, and went whistling all over the house, much pleased with my whistle, but disturbing all the family. My brothers, and sisters, and cousins, understanding the bargain I had made, told me I had given four times as much for the whistle as it was worth. They put me in mind what good things I might have bought with the rest of the money; and laughed at me so much for my folly, that I cried with vexation. The reflection of how much I had spent for the whistle now gave me more unhappiness than the whistle gave me pleasure.

This experience, however, was afterwards of use to me. Often, when I was tempted to buy some unnecessary thing, I said to myself, Don't give too much for the whistle; and I saved my money.

Over the years, as I grew up, came into the world, and observed the actions of others, I thought I met with many, very many, who gave too much for their whistles

When I saw a man spending all his energies in pursuit of fame and fortune, sacrificing his peace of mind, his honor, his friends, and even his family to attain them, I have said to myself, this man gives too much for his whistle.

If I knew a miser, who gave up every kind of comfortable living, all the pleasure of doing good to others, all the esteem of his fellow-citizens, and the joys of benevolent friendship, for the sake of accumulating wealth, Poor man, said I, you pay too much for your whistle.

When I met with a man obsessed with pleasure, sacrificing every worthwhile improvement of the mind, or of his fortune, to mere physical sensations, and ruining his health in their pursuit, Mistaken man, said I, you are providing pain for yourself, instead of pleasure; you give too much for your whistle.

If I see one fond of appearance, or fine clothes, fine houses, fine furniture, fine equipages, all above his fortune, for which he goes into debt, and ends his career bankrupt and broken, Alas! say I, he has paid dear, very dear, for his whistle.

When I see a beautiful, sweet-tempered girl married to an ill-natured brute of a husband, What a pity, say I, that she should pay so much for a whistle.

In short, I conceive that a great part of the miseries of mankind are brought upon them by the false estimates they have made of the value of things, and by their giving too much for their whistles.

Hindsight Questions
- Why did Benjamin Franklin become unhappy with his whistle?
- How was this experience beneficial to him in later life?
- What are some ways in which he felt people spend too much for their whistles?

Insight Questions
- What are some examples of people not wanting things that are good for them?
- What are some examples of people wanting things that are not good for them?
- How is it possible to spend too much for what we want?

Foresight Questions
- Why is it important to be thoughtful about the things you want?
- How can you avoid paying too much for your whistles?

Discussion Opportunity: Once Possessit gets the stirrings of desire going within us, Perverter can step in with his illusion befoggers and lead us to pay too much for our whistles. Puff Belarge and the thing we want seems so very important. Puff Belittle and we minimize or ignore the actual cost of what we want. We think we are spending one thing and discover we spent something else. Thus the man spending his energies in pursuit of fame and fortune frequently discovers fame and fortune illusive and if found, fickle and temporary. The miser discovers the cost of wealth to be the loss of friendships and ordinary pleasures. The man obsessed with pleasure discovers pleasure to be a demanding master who requires the person's wealth and health in return for an empty shell of a body and mind. The person fond of appearances discovers bankruptcy and poverty. And the beautiful girl who marries a brute who treats her poorly finds her love a very one sided and an emotionally costly affair. Thus all end up spending too much for their whistles, and ultimately discover themselves unhappy with their purchase. Character Traits: PR ownership; SR self-denial

ACTIVITY 8

QUOTH POOR RICHARD

Take each quote, one at a time and explore what each one means. Allow your students time to think about the message and then invite them to explain the meaning and provide specific examples of situations that illustrate the meaning of the quote.

Many a Man thinks he is buying Pleasure, when he is really selling himself a Slave to it. (1750

If Man could have half his wishes, he would double his troubles. (1752)

Is there anything Men take more pains about than to render themselves unhappy? (1738)

If what most men admire, they would despise, 'Twould look as if mankind were growing wise. (1735)

Many a Man would have been worse, if his Estate had been better. (1751)

Discussion Opportunity: Possessit has the ability to influence people to want things that aren't good for them. Remind the students Franklin wrote these things in the 1700's. These principles have been around for a long time and are not new. But many people fail to understand them. Character Traits: PR ownership; SR self-denial

ACTIVITY 9

HOW MUCH LAND DOES A MAN NEED?

Adapted from Leo Tolstoy's "How Much Land Does a Man Need"

ADVANCE PREPARATION: *Photocopy the quiz on page 23 for students.*
Instruct your students to listen carefully as you read this story as you will be giving them a written quiz afterwards.

Pahom pondered how much land he thought he would need to satisfy his yearnings to be wealthy. He had received what to him was a fantastic offer to acquire a great amount of land. A Chief of the Bashkirs had offered to sell him all the land he wanted at the price of one thousand rubles a day. Pahom did not understand.

"A day? What kind of measure is that? How many acres would that be?"

"We do know how else to reckon it," said the Chief. "We sell it by the day. For the price of one thousand rubles, you can have as much land as you can go round in one day."

Pahom was surprised.

"But in a day you can walk round a very large tract of land," he said.

The Chief laughed.

"True. And it will all be yours!" said he. "But there is one condition: If you do not return to the spot from where you started on the same day, your money is lost."

Pahom was delighted. They agreed he would start early next morning.

All night long Pahom lay awake pondering how much land he could mark off. "I can easily walk 35 miles in a day." he thought. Pahom was anxious to get going.

The next day, Pahom met the Chief at the appointed place, payed his one thousand rubles, quickly got started. He began by walking very rapidly, thinking to get as far as he could. But, the day was hot and after some hours Pahom grew very tired. Between the heat and his own anxiety,

Pahom was unable to rest properly. He thought to himself: "An hour to suffer, a life-time to live." Pahom was marking out a square piece of land and knew that after he had gone in one direction for a long time, he should turn and go to the left in order to arrive back on time. But when he saw a particularly rich piece of land, Pahom thought, "It would be a pity to leave that out," and continued in the same direction until he had included all of that piece of land. When Pahom finally looked at the sun, he suddenly realized it was setting rapidly. "What shall I do. . .have I tried to grasp too much?" He began running, as fast as he could, back toward the starting place. His lungs were searing, his breast was heaving like a blacksmith's bellows, his heart was pounding like a hammer, and his legs would hardly carry him forward. Seized with terror, Pahom feared he would not reach the starting point. Putting forth the last remnant of his strength and straining with every muscle, Pahom reached the starting place where the Chief was waiting for him just before sunset. As Pahom reached the mark, his legs gave way beneath him and he fell forward.

"Ah, what a fine fellow!" the Chief said, "He has gained very much land!"

Pahom's servant ran up to help him, but as he raised his head from the ground, he saw blood flowing from Pahom's mouth. Pahom was dead!

Picking up the spade, his servant dug a grave long enough for Pahom to lie in, and in it Pahom was buried. Six feet from his head to his heels. That's all the land Pahom needed.

Hindsight Questions
- What did you learn from this story?

Insight Questions
- How did Possessit influence Pahom's thinking?
- How did Perverter influence Pahom's thinking?
  What did he exaggerate or overvalue?
  What did he minimize or undervalue?

Foresight Questions
- What is the risk when we exaggerate the importance of something and underestimate its costs?

> **Discussion Opportunity:** Possessit convinced Pahom he needed more land. Perverter made it seem to Pahom that acquiring as much land as possible was the most important thing he could do. It took precedence over taking care of his family. It took precedence over everything else in life. The more land he had, he reasoned, the better things would be. The "I Want Bias" took over his reasoning capacity, he extended beyond his reach, and lost his life in the process. Character Traits: PR duty, accountability; SR self-denial

ACTIVITY 10

MAGNETIC NORTH

ADVANCE PREPARATION: *Invite one or more students to bring a magnetic compass and magnet to class.*

In class demonstrate how the compass will show which way is magnetic north. Point out that this can be an effective guide to a person in the wilderness who needs to be able to tell directions. However, the compass has a built in bias. It is influenced by the strongest magnetic field in proximity to the compass. Demonstrate how a magnet placed next to the compass may cause the compass to read north wherever the magnet is placed. In reality, a magnetic compass does not tell you which way is north, it merely tells you the direction of the strongest magnetic field influencing it. If that magnetic field is north, then we can keep our bearings, but if it is some other direction, then we can become lost.

> **Discussion Opportunity:** The "I Want Bias" is much like the magnetic field that influences this compass. The things we want most exert the strongest pull on our interests and attention and will have the greatest influence on our choices. When those wants are not consistent with our well being, we will go in directions that will not lead to happiness. Character Traits: PR ownership

How Much Land Does A Man Need?

TRUE OR FALSE

_____ Pahom was more interested in providing for the needs of his family than in satisfying his wants.

_____ One of Pahom's problems was that he did not appreciate the things he already had.

_____ Another problem Pahom had was in wanting more land than he could reasonably pay for.

_____ If Pahom had paid more attention to his needs, he would have been better able to satisfy his wants.

_____ If Pahom had known what the land would really cost, he would have still done what he did.

_____ Owning a large amount of land is always a greater benefit than owning a small amount of land.

_____ The Chief of the Bashkir's placed a higher value on one thousand rubles than he did on the land.

_____ In the end, Pahom received a great deal of benefit from the land he acquired.

_____ People always want things that are good for them.

_____ People sometimes spend a great deal of time, money, and effort to get things that do not benefit them.

_____ Where we spend our time, money, and effort is a good measure of what we think important.

How did each of the following agents of EPT influence Pahom?

ACTIVITY 11

SO CONVENIENT TO BE A REASONABLE CREATURE

from *Benjamin Franklin's The Art of Virtue*

"In my first voyage from Boston, being becalmed off Block Island, our people set about catching cod, and hauled up a great many. Hitherto, I had stuck to my [vegetarian diet] as I considered the taking of fish as a kind of unprovoked murder, since none of them had, or ever could do us any injury that might justify the slaughter. All this seemed very reasonable. But I had formerly been a great lover of fish, and when this came hot out of the frying-pan, it smelt admirably well. I balanced sometime between principle and inclination, till I recollected that, when the fish were opened, I saw smaller fish taken out of their stomachs; then thought I, 'If you eat one another, I don't see why we may'nt eat you.' So I dined upon cod very heartily, and continued to eat with other people, returning only now and then occasionally to a vegetable diet. *So convenient a thing it is to be a reasonable creature, since it enables one to find or make a reason for every thing one has a mind to do.*"

Hindsight Questions
• Why did Franklin say it was convenient to be a reasonable creature?

Insight Questions
• What did he mean by that?
• How do our wants influence our ability to reason?

Foresight Questions
• Why is it important to recognize that our wants can lead us to create reasons?

Discussion Opportunity: Possessit's primary mission is to infect people with the "I Want Bias." The "I Want Bias" is the tendency to create reasons to justify getting the things we want. This tendency is more or less operative in all people. But in some it can lead to disastrous results. The man who justifies robbing a bank because he wants some money is putting himself and others at serious risk of injury. The woman who justifies drinking to escape her problems is at risk of making her problems far worse than they were before. Character Traits: PR ownership, duty; SR self-understanding, self-denial

ACTIVITY 12

THE MIGHTY GENGHIS KHAN

A Tale of Anger and Remorse

Retold by George L. Rogers

A mighty king was Genghis Khan,
A powerful man was he,
He ruled from ancient Persia
Across the Yellow Sea.

The fate of millions hung in his grasp,
He ruled with brain and brawn,
And all men bended to his will,
This mighty Genghis Khan.

Now Genghis Kahn was fond of sport,
And so he trained a hawk,
To help him seek his favorite game,
Mid fir and field and rock.

It proved to be a faithful hawk,
And oft at early dawn,
It rode away upon the arm,
Of mighty Genghis Khan.

Now Genghis loved this loyal hawk,
As if a trusted friend,
Which makes this tale much sadder,
To hear its tragic end.

In search of game one fateful day,
The two had early gone,
With jolly friends who joined the hunt,
With mighty Genghis Khan.

The boisterous hunters enjoyed themselves,
A merry lot were they,
As they roamed across the fields,
And filled their bags with prey.

But as the heat bore down on them,
Their water long since gone,
To whet his thirst became the goal,
Of mighty Genghis Khan.

He found a stream with trickling flow,
And slowly filled his cup,
His thirst was great and with restraint,
He watched his cup fill up.

But before he drank his faithful hawk,
Swooped down and fell upon,
His arm and hand and spilled the cup,
Of mighty Genghis Khan.

Two more times this mighty king,
His goblet slowly filled,
And two more times the bird swooped down,
And on the ground it spilled.

An angry king the third time round,
Waited with long sword drawn,
No bird nor man dare trifle with,
This mighty Genghis Khan.

With powerful arm and lightning speed,
His sharp sword struck the bird,
Its lifeless form fell on the ground,
Then scarce a sound was heard.

Now in fray he lost his cup,
For it had fallen yon,
But this did not deter him,
Not mighty Genghis Khan.

He climbed the rock to reach the source,
From which the water rolled,
But in the pool he saw a sight,
Which made his blood run cold.

A poisonous snake lay in that pool,
Its life had long since gone,
And, had he drank, it would have killed,
The mighty Genghis Khan.

No longer did he think of thirst,
But only of his friend,
A faithful bird who saved his life,
To meet a tragic end.

He vowed a vow while standing there,
'Tis well to think upon,
"Never in anger will I strike again,"
Said mighty Genghis Khan.

Hindsight Questions
- Why did Genghis Khan lose his temper?
- What happened when he lost control?

Insight Questions
- Why did Genghis Khan vow to never strike in anger again?
- What is there about striking in anger that leads to tragedy?
- What is there about anger that causes us to lose control?
- How could the skill of Curiosity have helped Genghis Khan avoid this tragedy?

Foresight Questions
- Why is it important to be in control of your emotions before making important choices?
- What are some things you can do to gain control of your emotions when you are very upset?

Discussion Opportunity: Possessit along with a Puff Belarger from Perverter took Genghis Khan's desire for water to an intense level. When his favorite hawk interfered with his ability to satisfy his wants, Passionata inflamed Genghis Khan's temper to the level he killed his bird. It wasn't until he discovered the bird had saved his life he realized how rash he had been. Now, his desire for water was gone, but so was his faithful hawk. Under the influence of these agents of Error-Prone Thinking, many sad deeds are done and many regrets and sorrows are created. To avoid the kind of unhappiness created by making choices under their influence, it is necessary to develop mental safeguards to protect against them. For Genghis Khan, the safeguard to prevent his doing something like that again was a vow. Character Traits: PR accountability; SR self-denial; RO caring

ACTIVITY 13

WHAT ABOUT RYAN?

In the fall of 1984, Ryan White was an honors student at Western Middle School near Kokomo, Indiana. Although he suffered with a disease known as hemophilia, Ryan was a normal young boy, well-liked by his friends and well-accepted in his community. Ryan's illness required frequent blood transfusions and he had to spend considerable time in the hospital, but for the most part he led a normal life.

In September of 1984, Ryan began experiencing diarrhea, stomach cramps, and night sweats. His doctors thought he had a bad case of flu, but it did not get better and by December Ryan was suffering from chronic coughing and severe physical fatigue. After extensive testing Ryan was finally diagnosed as having AIDS. He had received the virus from one of his blood transfusions. After six years of near-constant illness, Ryan died in April of 1990.

The tragedy of Ryan's life, however, was not his physical suffering, though he suffered much, nor was it his early death, though he died very young. The real tragedy for Ryan was in how other people treated him when it was discovered that he had AIDS.

Shortly after Ryan was released from the hospital in February 1985, he and his family discovered some unforeseen problems which made it impossible for them to resume a normal life.

When Ryan was able to return to church, members of the congregation went to great lengths to keep their distance from he and his family. The next Sunday, Ryan was asked to sit in either the front or back row so everyone would know where he was at all times.

In July, Ryan was told he would not be allowed to return to school in the fall. School officials were afraid that he would infect the other children. Ryan was stung by the injustice of their decision. Doctors had explained to them that there was not any danger of other kids contracting the HIV virus from him. So Ryan decided to fight back, and persuaded his mother to file a law suit against the school. A "Concerned Citizens" committee then formed to keep him out of school. Public opinion against Ryan increased.

On their way home from the hospital one evening, Ryan and his mother stopped to eat in a restaurant. The owner happened to recognize them and refused to serve them water or any beverage in a glass. He would only serve them canned beverages. When they prepared to leave they heard him instruct the waitress to destroy the dishes they had used.

At work, other workers harassed Ryan's mother and vandalized her car. At home, vandals frequently threw trash on their lawn and eggs at their windows. Kids riding by on bicycles often shouted obscene names. Letters to the editor, printed in the local newspaper, accused Ryan of spitting on produce in local grocery stores, of biting and scratching other kids who wouldn't let him have his own way, and of urinating on the walls of public rest rooms.

Eventually, Ryan was reinstated back in school, but no longer could he attend as a normal student. The day he returned many parents kept their children at home. Kids accused him of being a murderer. They said other students would die because of him. He was required to eat on paper plates in the cafeteria and to use a separate water fountain and private toilet. As he walked down the halls, other kids would throw themselves against the lockers and holler "Look out, here he comes" as he walked by.

All of these experiences were in addition to Ryan's battle with AIDS, frequent trips to the hospital, and dealing with the physical effects of the disease. Of course, Ryan's family also had to deal with all of the same challenges that Ryan did.

Even after Ryan's death, vandals frequently toppled his tombstone and desecrated his grave site. It appears that for some, the prejudice and resentment against Ryan continued beyond his life.

Hindsight Questions
- What were the people in Ryan's home town afraid of?
- How did their fears influence their choices?
- How helpful were their choices to the Whites? To themselves?

Insight Questions
- How much understanding of AID's did the people in Ryan's home town really have?
- Why did people vandalize their home?
- Why did people generate lies and falsehoods about Ryan?

Foresight Questions
- What happens when people act on emotion without understanding?
- What can you do to avoid these kinds of fears and prejudices?

Discussion Opportunity: Perverter saw an opportunity and went to work. With blasts from the Puff Belarger and Puff Belittle befoggers the whole community grossly exaggerated the danger of AIDS and greatly minimized the needs of Ryan and his family. Motivated by exaggerated fears and operating with limited understanding they became easy prey for the Puff Prejudge befogger. In this mode of thinking many of them fell victim to Prevaricator and generated lies and additional false rumors that only inflamed their fears even more. Polarizer took them to the next step and they were convinced the White's were their enemies, justifying in their minds the performance all sorts of of cowardly, shameful, and even illegal acts. At this time and place, agents of EPT had tremendous success in undermining the civility of a whole community and creating a lot of unhappiness for many people. Character Traits: PR duty; SR self-understanding; RO caring, fairness, citizenship; T honesty

---

AIDS Facts

"Although [AIDS] is a very dangerous virus once it gets inside a person's body and starts multiplying, it isn't a very hearty virus at all outside the body. In fact, it is quite frail. It doesn't survive floating around in the air of a room. . .[or] when deposited on hard objects such as doorknobs, toilet seats, or eating utensils. It is effectively destroyed by most common detergents and disinfectants, including ordinary soap-and-water washing of the hands. . .The virus is not spread by coughing or sneezing or respiratory droplets the way cold and flu viruses are. You aren't going to acquire an AIDS infection from an infected person unless you have sexual contact with him or her, or are in intimate contact with that person's infected blood or other body fluids." Nourse, Alan E., M.D., AIDS, New York: Franklin Watts, 1990, page 111.

There are no known cases of HIV infection arising from casual contact. According to Mike Osterholm, state epidemiologist for the state of Minnesota, the risk of getting AIDS from someone like Ryan White is less than the risk of getting killed by a baseball, playing school sports, or getting on and off a school bus. According to Osterholm, "paramedics are often drenched in blood and body fluids, yet none is known to have acquired the virus from HIV-positive patients." Minneapolis Star and Tribune, March 24, 1992, page 8A.

ACTIVITY 14

THE LINES EXPERIMENT

ADVANCE PREPARATION: *Prepare an overhead of the lines graphic on page 30. Privately invite five students to participate. Explain that the object of the experiment is to demonstrate the influence of peer pressure. Show them the sheet with the lines and explain that on the day of class, there will be six students selected from the class to look at an overhead of these lines and to vote for which line in each set they think is longest. Instruct them that on third set of lines they are to vote that the bottom line is the longest. Explain that five of the six will have received this instruction, but one will not. The object is to see how the one will respond when the other five vote that the bottom line is the longest.*

In class, explain to your students that you will be showing an overhead with three sets of lines on it. Each set consists of two lines, one longer than the other. You are going to select six students to see if they can tell the longest line from the shortest line in each set. Invite the five students previously selected plus one other to come forward and face the screen. Place the overhead on the projector and ask the six students to take a moment and study the first set of lines. Then tell them that when you call them by name they are to tell you which line they think is longest. Then, starting with the the top set of lines first, ask each of the six students, one by one, to vote for which of the two lines, the top or bottom, they think is longest. When you get to the third set, ask the five who have been privately instructed to vote first, and the sixth person who has not been informed of the experiment to vote last.

Hindsight Questions
- What did you learn from this experiment?

Insight Questions
- Why is it difficult to go contrary to the crowd?
- How much influence do others have on our thoughts and feelings?
- To what extent are we influenced by television and other media?

Foresight Questions
- Why might it sometimes be necessary to go contrary to the crowd?

Discussion Opportunity: Peer pressure is a very real thing. Possessit gets us to think "I don't want to look stupid." and "I want to belong and be accepted by this group." Prevaricator then slips in to make us think, "They can't all be wrong, I must be mistaken." Then, we begin to doubt our own judgment and follow the crowd. But popular opinion is not always correct, acceptance is not always based on agreement, and one person may be able to help the others avoid making serious mistakes by expressing honest disagreement. Character Traits: PR ownership; T honest w/self

---

ACTIVITY 15

THOSE WHO BELIEVE IN INVISIBLE THREAD

Hans Christian Anderson's *The Emperor's New Clothes* Retold by George L. Rogers

The Emperor,
From his head to his toes,
Was constantly,
Dressed in the finest of clothes.

For he truly believed,
If believe this you can,
It's fashionable clothes
That make the man.

So he held frequent processions,
To show off his attire,
And prove to his subjects,
He was a king to admire.

One day, two swindlers,
Came to visit the King,
To tell him they had invented,
A most wonderful thing.

It was a magical thread,
Invisible to fools,
And therefore quite valuable,
To anyone who rules.

Said they to the King,
"With this thread thou can'st tell,
Who is fit for his post,
And who is dishonest as well.

"So to thy Highness,
The thing we propose,
Is to make thee a set,
Of the finest of clothes.

"Then thou can'st be certain,
There are no fools in thy court,
When thou seekest advice,
Of the most difficult sort.

"They will be exquisite,
In their elegance and beauty,
Yet, ever so helpful,
In fulfilling thy duty.

"For those who are foolish,
Will be unable to see,
The wonderful fabric,
We'll have woven for thee."

Filled with wonder and delight,
The king thought with a sigh,
"With such beautiful garments,
Who could be wiser than I?"

And so, for a princely sum,
He hired this nefarious pair,
To weave him some clothes,
From nothing but air.

Then high in the castle,
He ordered a room,
Prepared for the weavers,
Their thread and their loom.

Soon, these two scoundrels,
With a smile and a smirk,
Had their loom humming,
And were busy at work.

Clack, clack, swish, swish,
Hour after hour, and into the night,
They worked day after day,
With all of their might.

After some time,
The King wanted to know,
How the work was progressing,
How fast or how slow.

But afraid he could not see,
This invisible thread,
He sent his wisest minister,
To go in his stead.

"Ah, wonderful, marvelous,"
The minister said with a stare,
Though there was nothing to see,
But only thin air.

For the thing the minister,
Feared first and foremost,
Was to admit he saw nothing,
And was unfit for his post.

So he reported to the King,
With a wave of his hand,
"Thy new clothes are exquisite,
They're beautiful and grand."

"Splendid," cried the King,
"Then, we shall have a parade,
In which my new clothes,
Shall be grandly displayed."

So the date was set,
For only two weeks away,
And anxiously the King's subjects,
Awaited the day.

Frequently the King,
With his ministers, and queen,
Now visited the weavers,
To see what could be seen.

"Marvelous, exquisite,
and wonderful," they all said,
"Are these beautiful garments,
Made from this magnificent
thread."

So day after day,
Never leaving their room,
The weavers kept weaving,
Thin air on their loom.

While all the King's subjects,
Anxiously waited to see,
The Emperor's new clothes,
And how beautiful they'd be

When the day finally came,
People lined up the street,
For all wanted to see,
This spectacular treat.

While back in the castle,
Our unscrupulous pair,
Were carefully dressing,
The King in thin air.

"The fabric is so light,"
Said they to the King,
"You will feel like you are naked,
And not wearing a thing.

"But isn't it beautiful,
And wonderful to behold,
With the intricate patterns,
And the colors so bold?"

"Um, yes," mumbled the King,
For the thing he feared most,
They would think him a fool,
And unfit for his post.

Soon procession got started,
With everyone in place,
Courtiers and Pages,
All surrounding his Grace.

Gasps and "Oh My's",
Were heard as he came into sight,
With each viewer pretending,
It was a gasp of delight.

Ohhh's and Ahhh's,
All followed the King,
For no one would acknowledge,
He was not wearing a thing.

Until a small child,
Who didn't understand,
Invisible clothes,
And things equally grand.

Said, "Mother, he's naked,
The King has no clothes,
He has nothing on,
From his head to his toes."

"My son, you are right."
The child's mother said,
And from one to another,
The word quickly spread.

"The King is quite naked,
As naked can be.
He has no clothes on,
Can't you see, can't you see?"

And while the crowd stood there,
With their mouths all agape,
The two rascally scoundrels,
Quickly made their escape.

But, in time, some good came,
From this unfortunate affair,
When the King finally realized,
You are more than you wear.

And so he made a decision,
On which he made good,
To become the best Emperor,
That he possibly could.

And his subjects were eager,
To forgive and forget,
For all had been foolish,
All had to admit.

"There is nothing," said they,
In which to be proud,
"If all that one does,
Is to follow the crowd.

"For of the person who does,
The best that can be said,
Is that he likely believes,
In invisible thread."

Hindsight Questions:
- What did the King want to possess?
- What are some lies the King chose to believe?

Insight Questions:
- Why was the King vulnerable to to the lies told by the swindlers?

Foresight Questions:
- Why is it risky to allow ourselves to be too easily influenced by the opinions of others?

Discussion Opportunity: After Possessit convinced the king he wanted to be admired, Prevaricator convinced him all he needed was fashionable clothes. The first lie Prevaricator convinced the King of was that clothes make the person. With this idea in mind, he was vulnerable the lie that clothing woven with invisible thread could make him wise. In their desire to be thought fit for their positions, the King's ministers bought into the lie as well. It was an innocent child who, by simply acknowledging what he saw, brought everyone to their senses. Character Traits: PR ownership, duty, accountability; T honesty

ACTIVITY 16

THE MARTYRDOM OF ANDY DRAKE

by Ben Burton

Andy Drake was a sweet, innocent and amusing little guy whom everyone liked. They also heckled him. During these many years, I've asked myself why we did it. . . . . Were we simply unthinking?. . . .

He took the kidding well and always smiled back with those great big eyes which seemed to say "thank you" with each sweeping blink. Perhaps he was saying, "I'm happy to have even the crumbs from the table." When any of us fifth graders needed to vent our frustrations, he was willing to pay the price for membership in our group.

We had a verse which we chanted:
    Andy Drake don't eat no cake,
    And his Ma don't eat no pie.
    If it wasn't for that welfare dole
    All those Drakes would surely die.

As I said, I don't know why Andy had to pay this special fee for membership in our group. I don't recall that any of us ever mentioned that Andy's father was in prison, or that his mother took in washing. Or that any of us noticed the sadness and embarrassment in her eyes as she looked at you.

Snobbery blossoms very young. I say this because it's plain now that our attitude was that it was right for the rest of us to belong to the group but that Andy was there by our sufferance.

But we all really liked Andy—liked him, that is until that day—until that moment. Our rationale in making the decision the way we did was that "he's different." "We don't want him do we?" someone said. Which one of us said it? At first I wanted to blame Jeff. But I can't honestly say that I remember who said it—who spoke those words

that brought out the savagery lying dormant in all of us. It doesn't matter, because the fervor with which we all took up the cry revealed us— revealed us every one.

This weekend was to be like so many others the group had enjoyed together. After school on Friday we would meet at one of our homes—this time mine—to prepare for a camp out in the nearby woods. Our mothers, who made most of the preparations, always fixed an extra sack for Andy who joined us after he had done his chores.

By the time we made camp, mother's apron strings were forgotten; we were men against the jungle. The others told me that since it was my party, I should be the one to let Andy know he wasn't invited. . . . .

I can still see Andy as he came toward us down the long, dark tunnel of trees which let in only enough of the late evening light to kaleidoscope the changing designs on his old sweatshirt. He was on his rusty bike—a girl's model, with tires made of garden hose wired to the rims. He appeared happier than I had ever seen him, this little guy who had been an adult all of his life and who was now finding in the group his first chance to relax and have a little fun.

He waved to me as I stood in the camp clearing. I ignored his greeting. He climbed off his bike and trotted over to me, full of conversation. The others, well concealed inside the tent, were completely quiet; but I could almost hear them listening and breathing.

Why won't he get serious? I asked myself. Can't he see that I am not returning his gaiety?

Then suddenly he did see; his innocent countenance opened even more, leaving him totally vulnerable and exposed. His whole demeanor said, "It's going to be very bad isn't it? But let's have it." Undoubtedly well-practiced in being disappointed, he didn't even brace for the blow.

Incredulously, I heard myself saying, "Andy, we don't want you."

Still hauntingly vivid is the stunning quickness with which two huge tears sprang to his eyes and just stayed there. I say "vivid" because I have had a million maddening reruns of the scene in my soul. . . .

Finally, a fleeting little tremor broke across his lips, and he turned away without protest. He stumbled at first, half stunned. Then he ran to his bike and rode quickly away.

As I entered the tent someone—the last one of us to feel the full charge of the moment, I guess—started singing the old verse:
Andy Drake don't eat no cake,
And his Ma. . . .

And then we all stopped. It was unanimous. No vote was taken, no word was spoken, but we all knew. We knew we had done something horribly, cruelly wrong. In that moment we felt an understanding new to us but now indelibly fixed upon our souls. We had martyred an individual. . . .with the only weapon against which he had no defense—rejection.

Andy's poor attendance at school made it difficult to tell when he actually withdrew, but one day it dawned upon me that he was no longer there. The fact that he was gone magnified my pain a million times. After the incident, whenever I'd seen him, I had managed to avoid him. But now I realized I had spent too many days struggling with myself to develop the proper way of telling him how totally, consummately ashamed I was. I had lost my chance to make it right to him. Now I know that to have embraced Andy and to have cried with him would have been enough.

Hindsight Questions
- What kind of a boy was Andy?
- What label did the other boys place on Andy?
- How did the author feel about how they treated Andy?

Insight Questions
- Why did the author feel ashamed of what they had done?
- Why is it impossible to build yourself up by tearing others down?
- What did the author discover was really important to him?

Foresight Questions
- Why is it important to be considerate of other's feelings?
- What benefit is there in befriending the underdog?

Discussion Opportunity: All the boys wanted acceptance by the group. Unfortunately, Perverter let loose all his befoggers on the other boys and Andy never had a chance. Puff Belarger and they had the illusion they were somehow better than Andy. Puff Prejudge and Andy was unworthy of their association. Puff Belittle and his feelings did not matter. Puff Belabeled Andy was designated as a welfare person and therefore of lesser value than other people. Polarizer stepped in, it was them against him. Andy lost. But the boys lost too. Perhaps even more. These are the kinds of tragedies that occur when people yield to the EPT's. Character Traits: PR ownership, accountable; RO caring, fairness, citizenship

---

ACTIVITY 17

WHAT'S IN A NAME?

17-1 The Montagues and the Capulets

Romeo was a Montague by birth, Juliet a Capulet. Long before they were born, and for reasons no longer known, their families were mortal enemies. Unfortunately, Romeo and Juliet were in love. One evening, Romeo secretly comes to Juliet's home to declare his love and seek her hand in marriage. Following is part of this famous scene.

Jul. O Romeo, Romeo! wherefore art thou
    Romeo?
Deny thy father and refuse thy name;
Or, if thou wilt not, be but my sworn love,
And I'll no longer be a Capulet.
    Rom. [Aside] Shall I hear more or speak at
    this?
Jul. 'Tis but thy name that is my enemy;
Thou art thyself, though not a Montague.
What's a Montague? it is nor hand, nor foot,
Nor arm, nor face, nor any other part
Belonging to a man. O, be some other name!
What's in a name? that which we call a rose
By any other name would smell as sweet;
So, Romeo would, were he not Romeo call'd,
Retain that dear perfection which he owes
Without that title. Romeo, doff thy name,
And for that name which is no part of thee
Take all myself. . . .
How camest thou hither, tell me. . . .
If any of my kinsmen find thee here.
    Rom. With love's light wings did I o'er-perch
    these walls. . . .

Therefore thy kinsmen are no let to me.
Jul. If they do see thee, they will murder thee.

The next day, Romeo and Juliet secretly exchange marriage vows, but to them, the privilege of living happily after was not given. Later that same day the feud between the two families erupts again, this time involving Romeo. Tybalt, a cousin of Juliet provokes a duel with Romeo, but only after killing Romeo's best friend. Romeo, in turn, kills Tybalt. For this act, Romeo is to be banished from Verona. In the mean time, Juliet's father pledges Juliet to Count Paris, and when she refuses, is told he will disown her.

So she won't have to marry the Count, Juliet takes a potion that makes it appear she is dead and sends a message to Romeo explaining what she has done. Unfortunately, Romeo does not get her message and thinking Juliet is dead, does not wish to live any longer himself. So, Romeo drinks some real poison. When Juliet finds out that Romeo is dead, she too, no longer wishes to live and takes her own life. Now both are dead.

In the concluding scene, both Lord Capulet and Lord Montague are grief stricken as they realize their feud has caused the death of the people they loved most. Knowing the feuding between the two families must end, Lord Capulet holds out his hand in friendship to Lord Montague who accepts the offer.

Hindsight Questions
- Why did Romeo and Juliet have to meet and get married in secret?
- What finally ended the feud between the two families?
- How did the feud between the two families contribute to the deaths of Romeo and Juliet?

Insight Questions
- What did Juliet mean when she said, "Tis but thy name that is my enemy"?
- How does the labeling of people and groups lead to conflict between groups?

Foresight Questions
- What are the natural consequences of polarized thinking?

17-2 The Jets and the Sharks

West side Story is a musical play about two rival street gangs in New York City, the Jets and the Sharks. The Jets are native New Yorkers. The Sharks are Puerto Ricans who have moved to New York. The Jets are led by Riff, the Sharks by Bernardo. Riff and Bernardo hold a war council and agree to a fight between the two gangs to decide once and for all who controls a two block area they each call their turf.

Tony, Riff's best friend, is a former Jet who is trying to make something of himself and has quit the gang scene. Maria, Bernardo's beautiful younger sister and Tony meet at a local dance and fall in love. When Bernardo finds out, he is furious and forbids Maria to have anything to do with Tony. But Tony and Maria see only each other and cannot be kept apart.

Riff wants Tony to join with the Jets in the fight. Tony refuses. But on the night of the rumble, Maria afraid someone will be hurt, asks Tony to go and stop the fight. Tony tries, but when Bernardo sees Tony, he starts pushing Tony

around. Riff steps in. He and Bernardo fight. The fight was to be skin on skin, but both pull knives. Caught up in the savagery of the moment, each slash at the other and, in the scuffle, Riff trips and falls into Bernardo's knife. In a fit of rage, Tony grabs Riff's knife and thrusts it into Bernardo, killing him. Gang members, filled with the horror of the scene, flee in all directions.

Tony, overcome with grief makes his way back to Maria and tells her what happened. Deciding they need to get away, Tony leaves Maria to go get some money. Shortly after, Tony is told that Chino, Bernardo's best friend has killed Maria and is looking for him with a gun. No longer wanting to live, Tony calls for out Chino to kill him too. Maria, still very much alive, learns that Chino is looking for Tony and runs to warn him. Maria and Chino find Tony at the same time. As Maria rushes to Tony's side, Chino fires his gun and kills Tony.

Hindsight Questions
- What were the Sharks and Jets fighting for?
- How did their group memberships influence how they felt about one another?

Insight Questions
- Why did each group hate the other?
- How did the labels "Jets" and "Sharks" contribute to the conflict?
- What did they do that allowed Passionata to have such a large influence on them?

Foresight Questions
- Why is polarization a mutually destructive mentality?

17-3 What Do These Groups Have in Common?

Assign individuals to select one of the following groups and research the nature of the conflict between the opposing sides of each group. Ask them to consider what the quarrel is or was about, how serious the quarrel has been, and the effect of the quarrel on members of each side.

Hatfields and McCoys
The Catholics and the Protestants in Ireland
Israel and Palestine
Croats and Serbs
Grangerfords and Shephardsons in Huckleberry Finn
Hindus and Muslims

Hindsight Questions
- What identified one group from another?
- How did members of one group think about members of the other group?
- What was/is the reason for conflict between the two groups?
- How did they treat each other?

Insight Questions
- How did the names make the people feel? About themselves? About each other?
- What did the names really tell them about each other?
- How does/did their names contribute to their animosity for one another?

Foresight Questions
- What can you learn from the experiences of these people?

Discussion Opportunity: The names for each of the above groups became labels that identified members of the same group as friends and members of the other group as enemies. Members of each group have quarreled, fought, and even killed members of the opposite group for no other reason than the fact they were labeled a member of that group. The cause for conflict between the different groups varies. For the Hatfields and McCoys, no one remembers. If you were a Hatfield, any McCoy was your enemy and visa versa. That's just the way it was. The quarrels between the other groups range from land to religion and from politics to appearance, but the real issue is always one group seeking predominance over the other. In all cases, once the label was attached, anyone bearing the opposite label was an enemy and having named the enemy, it became possible for one group to blame the other group for all their problems. Membership in some groups is voluntary, but in most, it is simply the result of birth. Without knowing anything about the hopes, dreams, interests, talents, concerns and cares of each other babies were born as enemies and taught to hate each other. Such is the power of Perverter's Puff Benamed Puff Beblamed befogger and of Polarizer. Character Traits: RO right, ownership, duty, accountability; SR self-understanding; RO caring, fairness, citizenship

ACTIVITY 18

DISCRIMINATION ACTIVITY

Identify students with blue eyes, separate them from the rest of the class, and pin a tag on each person. Explain that from now on, anyone with blue eyes will be considered inferior to other students. They will not be entitled to the same privileges as other students. They may not ask questions in class. They will be required to do extra work during recess and lunch breaks. If they talk back they will be punished.

Play it out for a bit and then discuss how those being discriminated against felt, and why. After some discussion read this description of life in Holland during WWII.

The true horror of German occupation came slowly. A rock thrown through a window here, an ugly word scrawled on the wall of a synagogue there, name calling and taunting of children in the school yard were were all signs of what was coming, but it was not clear at first. Then one day there was a sign on a local shop window, "No Jews Allowed." The next day, similar signs appeared on several shops. Then followed signs on the public library, restaurants, theaters and even the concert hall. Not long thereafter, men, women, and children were required to wear bright yellow stars attached to their coats and jacket fronts. In the center of each six pointed star was the word *Jood* (Jew). Next began the disappearances, a house mysteriously deserted, a shop closed and the apartment above abandoned.

Whether these people had been spirited away by the Gestapo or gone into hiding was unknown. Then one day, "as Father and I were returning from our daily walk we found the Grote Markt cordoned off by a double ring of police and soldiers. A truck was parked in front of the fish mart; into the back were climbing men, women, and children, all wearing the yellow star."

Adapted from the Hiding Place by Corrie Ten Boom

Hindsight Questions
- What label was attached to the people in our class activity?
- What label was attached to the people in the story of WWII?

Insight Questions
- How much did these labels (blue eyes and jew) really tell you about the people involved?
- How did the label jew influence how these people were treated?
- How fair do you think it is to treat people differently because of a label that has been given them?

Foresight Questions
- Why is it important to recognize the harmful aspects of labeling and name calling?
- What can you do to avoid being involved in this kind of activity?

Discussion Opportunity: In his book Mein Kampf, Hitler blamed the Jewish people for Germany's loss of WWI. According to Hitler, Germany had not lost the war in the field, but had been stabbed in the back by traitors at home. And who were these traitors? They were the Jews who controlled the production and finance of the war. Thus having named and blamed them as enemies, Hitler justified, in his own mind, the sending of millions of people by that name to their deaths. Such is the influence of the befogger, Puff Benamed Puff Beblamed. Character Traits: PR right, accountability; RO caring, fairness

---

ACTIVITY 19

THE NATURE OF THINGS

For the following quizzes, have your students number a paper one through ten. Explain that you are going to read them some statements about things many people believe. They are to write a "T" or "F" for each statement depending on whether they think it is true or false.

19-1   What Does Mother Nature Say?

1. Bamboos are trees.
2. The peanut is not really a nut.
3. Bats are very useful to have around.
4. Lightning never strikes the same place twice.
5. Smarter people have bigger brains.
6. There's an earthquake somewhere every day.
7. The arctic is a frozen wasteland.
8. Moths eat clothes.
9. The sky is blue.
10. A rain drop is pear shaped.

Answers for What Does Mother Nature Say?

1. F. Although bamboo plants may sometimes be as tall as a twelve story building, bamboo is really a grass.
2. T. The peanut is a member of the pea family.
3. T. Many bats are big insect eaters - as many as 150 mosquitoes for dinner. Others eat nectar and help pollinate plants.
4. F. The Eiffel Tower in Paris has been struck many times by lightning, sometimes several times during the same storm. This is true of many large structures.
5. F. There is no relationship between the size of a person's brain and intelligence.
6. T. In fact, every minute an earthquake takes place somewhere on our planet.
7. F. Although the arctic is a cold place, some parts actually have summer crops and certain areas of the arctic experience temperatures between 85-90 degrees Fahrenheit in the summer.
8. F. The mouth of a moth is a soft tube that cannot bite into clothing. The caterpillar of the clothes moth, however, will eat large holes in coats, sweaters, and other clothing.
9. F. Dust particles and water droplets in the air create the blueness we see, but above the atmosphere the sky is black.
10. F. High speed cameras reveal that a rain drop is donut shaped with a hole that doesn't quite go through it.

19-2   Natural Killers

1. Octopuses are not dangerous to people.
2. Gorillas will attack without warning.
3. Several people are killed by wolves every year.
4. Sharks frequently attack and kill swimmers.
5. A tarantula bite is poisonous and can kill you.
6. Killer Whales attack people in small boats.
7. Vampire Bats don't really exist.
8. Scorpions are very dangerous to people.
9. Grizzly bears are natural enemies of humans.
10. There is good reason to be afraid of spiders.

Answers to Natural Killers

1. T. Octopuses do not suck blood, their tentacles are not strong enough to hold a person, and they are very shy of people.
2. F. Gorillas scare enemies away by beating on themselves and the ground. They rarely attack people.
3. F. There are no known instances of a healthy wolf killing anyone in North America. Attacks by rabid wolves are rare.
4. F. There are about 100 shark attacks reported from around the world each year. Only 12 in the US. Compare this to 600 cases of people being struck by lightning each year in the US.
5. F. North American tarantulas will only bite in self-defense and their bite is no more serious than a bee sting.
6. F. There is not a single documented case of a killer whale attacking and killing a human being.
7. F. Vampire bats do exist. But they are not blood suckers. They prick the skin of cows, etc. and lap the blood.
8. T&F. A few kinds of scorpions in Arizona and Mexico are poisonous enough to kill a person, but most have a sting like a bee.
9. F. Grizzly bears usually only attack people for one of three reasons, a female protecting her cubs, they are surprised and are defending themselves, or are hungry and believe people have food.
10. F. Of some 30,000 different kinds of spiders in the world, about twelve are dangerous to people. In North America, only two have bites that can make a person very sick, the black widow spider and the brown recluse.

Reference Books for *The Nature of Things*

Cross Your Fingers, Spit in Your Hat by Alvin Schwartz, published by J.B. Lippincott
Don't Sing Before Breakfast, Don't Sleep in the Moonlight by Lila Perl, published by Clarion Books
'Old Wives' Tales, the Truth Behind Common Notions by Sue Castle, published by Citadel Press
The Simon and Schuster Book of Facts and Fallacies by Roda and Leda Blumberg, published by Simon and Schuster
The Unhuggables, the Truth about Snakes, Slugs, Spiders, and Other Animals that are Hard to Love published by the National Wildlife Foundation.

Hindsight Questions
- How many answered all questions correctly?
- Were there any questions everyone missed?

Insight Questions
- How do incorrect opinions get to be commonly believed?
- How important is correct information in forming a correct opinion?

Foresight Questions
- Why is it important to question what we believe from time to time?
- What are some ways we can check on the accuracy of our opinions?

Discussion Opportunity: Nature, not opinion, determines whether something is true or false. Even the reference books and the answers provided above do not present the whole truth. It is so easy, when we get a little information, or have someone we believe tell us something, to think we know all we need to know on a given subject. This is what Puff Prejudge tries to get us to think. If he can get us to form opinions based on false or insufficient information, he can lead us to make bad choices. Character Traits: RO duty; T dependability

ACTIVITY 20

QUOTH THE PHILOSOPHER

Take each quote, one at a time, and explore what each one means. Allow your students time to think about the message and then invite them to explain what the quote means and provide specific examples of situations that illustrate the meaning.

Artemus Ward
It ain't so much the things we don't know that get us into trouble. It's the things we know that just ain't so.

Josh Billings
I honestly believe it iz better tew know nothing than tew to know what ain't so.

Michel De Montaigne
Nothing is so firmly believed as what we least know.
Men are most apt to believe what they least understand.

Hubbard
The recipe for perpetual ignorance is: be satisfied with your opinions and content with your knowledge.

Discussion Opportunity: Just because we believe something doesn't make it true. It takes a great deal more effort to arrive at an understanding of the truth than it does to simply form an opinion. However, if our opinions are based on falsehoods or incorrect information, it is difficult to make good choices. Character Traits: PR duty, ownership, accountability; SR self-reliance; T dependability

CHOOSING TO DEVELOP THE SEVEN C SKILLS FOR THINKING CLEARLY

Section Two

LEARNING OBJECTIVES FOR SECTION TWO

Understand what the Seven C Skills are and their importance

Possess a knowledge of how to develop the Seven C Skills

Possess a desire to develop the Seven C Skills

SECTION OVERVIEW

In *The Descent of Man,* Charles Darwin wrote, "The highest possible stage in moral culture is when we recognize that we ought to control our thoughts. . . .Whatever makes any bad action familiar to the mind, renders its performance so much the easier." Unfortunately, thoughts that uplift, inspire, motivate, and encourage us to be better human beings seem to require greater effort than do contrary thoughts. To guide our thoughts to higher ground requires a strength of mind that is something more than I.Q. In his book by the same name, Daniel Goleman refers to this strength of mind as "emotional intelligence." Emotional intelligence is the ability to manage or control our thoughts and feelings and guide them to positive outcomes. To acquire this kind of mental and emotional strength requires a sustained and disciplined effort. It is not an accident of birth. Conscious choices must be made. One of these choices is the decision to develop seven specific thinking skills—Criticism, Concentration, Curiosity, Creativity, Communication, Control, and Correction.

Criticism: The ability to consider, study, question, compare, and form accurate judgments as to the value or worth of things

Concentration: The ability to pay close attention and stay on task

Curiosity: The ability to wonder, inquire, explore, and seek out new information

Creativity: The ability to imagine, originate, invent, and design new things

Communication: The ability to share ideas and knowledge through listening, speaking, reading, and writing

Control: The ability to govern one's own thoughts and feelings

Correction: The ability to make necessary changes in one's beliefs, choices, and actions to improve the results

The Seven C Skills are largely available to anyone who wishes to acquire them. *Desire and effort are far more important than intellectual capacity.* Therefore, it is necessary to help young people: 1) Understand the importance of acquiring these seven skills, 2) Know how to develop them, and 3) Commit to a life-long process of skill development that will greatly challenge them, but will also take them to otherwise unachievable heights of accomplishment and personal satisfaction.

ACTIVITY 21

MEET THE CLEAR THINKING TEAM

21-1 CT Intelligence Briefing

ADVANCE PREPARATION: *Photocopy the CT Intelligence Briefing Scripts on pages 48-50 to be read by eight students plus yourself. Prepare an overhead transparency of the CT Team on page 51 or have readers refer to the CT Team poster in presenting each of the Seven C Skills. If possible give the reading assignments in advance of class so each individual has a chance to practice a little. You may wish to take this section in segments having 3 to 5 readers participate in each segment.*

Start the presentation by saying:

Today, we will begin raising your capabilities to combat the influence of EPT to a new level by introducing you to Seven C Skills necessary for recognizing and resisting EPT activity in your operational units. We begin today's briefing with a brief introduction and instructions from (name of reader 1)

Hindsight Questions
- What are the Seven C's of Thinking Clearly?
- Who can learn the Seven C Skills?

Insight Questions
- Why are the Seven C Skills important to you?
- Why is desire a necessary requirement for developing the Seven C Skills?

Foresight Questions
- How can the Seven C Skills help make life better for you?
- How long do you think it will take to learn the Seven C Skills?

Discussion Opportunity: There are few things that have greater pay back than developing your thinking skills. The ability to think and reason is perhaps the highest capacity of human beings. But it is not always an advantage. Though our reasoning capacity enables us to do marvelous things no other creature can do, it also enables us to get into more mischief and trouble than any other creature. Although Benjamin Franklin was one of the brightest and most intellectually gifted men to ever live, he had a profound distrust of human reasoning, both his own and others. To help him avoid the problems of faulty reasoning or error-prone thinking, he developed several safeguards. Among them was a love of truth. Before forming an opinion on anything, he tried to make sure he clearly understood the facts. In addition to his own investigations, he actively sought out the opinions of others. Whenever he found he was in the wrong, he was quick to acknowledge his error and correct his opinion. Throughout his life he was a keen observer of others and sought to learn from their experiences and avoid their mistakes. In addition he actively developed his skills of concentration, curiosity, creativity, communication, and self-control—in other words he deliberately developed the Seven C Skills for Thinking Clearly. (See activities 24-1,2) Character Traits: PR ownership; SR self-reliance

21-2 The CT Quiz

ADVANCE PREPARATION: *Photocopy the CT Skills Quiz on pages 52 for your students. Hand out the quiz for students to complete.*

Hindsight Questions
- What have you learned so far about the Seven C Skills for Thinking Clearly?

Insight Questions
- In looking at the Seven C Skills, which ones do you think come most easily to you?
- Which ones do you think will require more work?

Foresight Questions
- How do you think these skills may be of help to you?

21-2 Things I Can Do to Develop the Seven C Skills

ADVANCE PREPARATION: *Photocopy the activity sheet on page 53 for each student.*

In class, divide students into small groups and allow them five minutes to brainstorm and come up with at least four things they can do individually, or you can do as a class, to actively develop each of the C skills. After the allotted time, take each skill and have each group present their ideas of things they can do to develop these skills. For those things that are individual, encourage them to prioritize the ones they think are most important and develop a plan for working on them. For those ideas that apply to the class, prioritize those that are most important and discuss how you might implement them in class.

Hindsight Questions
- Which of the C skills seem easiest to develop? Why?

Insight Questions
- What will it take individually for you to develop these skills?
* What will it take for us as a class to develop these skills?

Foresight Questions
- How do you think these skills will be helpful to you?
- Why is it important to make the effort to develop them?

Discussion Opportunity: Developing the C skills is a life long learning process. But the sooner begun the better, for the possession of these skills pays big dividends at every level of achievement. Fortunately, with a little attention, these are skills you can work at on a daily basis. It's fairly easy because they are skills you can use on a daily basis in virtually everything you do. The most important factor is desire. The next is having some method for consistently working on them, such as focusing on one skill a week, or one skill a day. Developing the C skills is not a casual effort, but the benefits of better choices and happier results, far exceed the effort. Character Traits: PR; SR; RO; T

CT Intelligence Briefing Scripts

Reader 1

Now that you have been introduced to the agents and tactics of EPT, it is time to begin a skill development program designed to help you overcome their insidious influence in areas for which you have operational responsibility. You will be trained in seven specific skills. They are the Seven C Skills for Thinking Clearly. Each of you already possess these skills to some degree. However, it is unlikely you possess any of them to the degree necessary to provide you effective safeguards against EPT. It is also unlikely you will know how to effectively employ them in recognizing and overcoming attempts by particular EPT agents to infiltrate your operations. As members of an elite counterintelligence unit, you not only need this training for your own protection, but also so you can give assistance to individuals you associate with who may not have had this training. Today you are going to receive an overview of the Seven S Skills. Seven members of your unit have each been asked to present a brief description of one of these skills, what it is and why it is important. Before we have their reports, however, our Chief would like to say a few words. Mr./Ms (name of teacher)

Teacher

Before we talk about the C skills, I would like to take a minute to talk about DESIRE. While the C skills may be mastered by anyone who wants to learn them, they will never be mastered by any one who doesn't want to make the effort. Desire, opportunity, and effort are the only requirements. I will be providing the opportunity. You must supply the desire and effort. If you have the desire, the effort will follow. I will try to make it interesting and hopefully fun, but interesting or not, fun or not, these are skills that pay big dividends to anyone who possesses them. If you have begun to pick up some on the dangers of EPT, hopefully you will also have begun to experience some desire to avoid them. However, the wonderful thing about the C skills is that they are not only defensive or protective, they are also proactive skills that can help you achieve almost any important goal in your life. If at any point you feel your desire is not as strong as you think it should be, let's talk. Ok, now let me turn you over to our first specialist who will introduce you to the C skill of Criticism. (*Name of Reader 1*).

Reader - Criticism
(Point to the Criticism Icon on the overhead or poster.)

Criticism is your first line of defense in protecting you from agents of EPT. Criticism enables you understand the nature of things. It also requires that you use the standard of truth and reason to measure the worth of things. Criticism also gives you the ability to detect falsehoods spread by Prevaricator and attempts to distort reality by Perverter.

Criticism gives you the ability to collect, observe, compare, analyze, and evaluate information. Let me give you a specific example of how the skill of Criticism works.

Suppose I see someone with a really cool pair of shoes that I really like. Note: Possessit is starting to work on me. So I ask the person where he/she got the shoes. I go to the store where the shoes are sold and find they cost $89. I have enough money to buy them, but if I do I won't be able to get some other things I need. Possessit will try to get me to just buy the shoes without thinking about anything else. But Criticism will cause me to think about what is really most important to me, the shoes or the other things I need. Criticism will cause me to collect information about what things cost and analyze what would be the best thing to do. It will help me make comparisons of each thing, and evaluate which is most important for me to have. This is how the skill of Criticism works. Now (*name of reader*) is going to tell you about the skill of Concentration.

Reader - Concentration
(Point to the Concentration Icon on the overhead or poster.)

Concentration is a skill that is required for the mastery of all difficult tasks. From learning to walk to flying an airplane, from learning to throw a ball to to weaving a basket, from learning to grow corn to performing heart surgery, Concentration is an essential skill to have. All of the other C skills draw on Concentration to reach their full potential.

Concentration is the ability to focus or fix your attention on a specific object or task long enough to master it. Concentration is the key to any real accomplishment in this life. EPT agents will do anything they can to interfere with your ability to develop or use this skill.

Now the key to Concentration is interest. As you know, it is difficult to concentrate on something that does not interest you. When you find areas that naturally interest you, recognize these as areas that you may be able to really excel in as it will be easier for you to concentrate on what you need to know. However, there will likely be things you need to know that are not of natural interest to you. These are areas where you will need to work on your concentration skills. To help, you may need to draw on other C skills such as Curiosity and Creativity. So let's have *(name of reader)* talk to you about Curiosity.

Reader - Curiosity
(Point to the Curiosity Icon on the overhead or poster.)

Curiosity's specialty is cutting through lies of Prevaricator and the befoggers of Perverter. A few good questions can dispel myths, clarify issues, and remove confusion. Both Criticism and Creativity rely heavily on Curiosity, and neither skill can be fully developed without it.

Curiosity is the ability to investigate, explore, and seek out new information. It is as important to personal growth and progress as it is to an effective defense against the EPT's. Curiosity is essentially the art of asking questions. It is the desire to know and understand the nature of things. The wonderful thing about Curiosity is that once you get it going it literally pulls you to all sorts of new information and understanding. Remember, there are no uninteresting things, only uninterested people. If you will use the six questions you leaned as a small child, Who? What? Why? How? Where? and When?, you will find they can make almost any topic interesting. Now let's go to Creativity. *(name of reader)*

Reader - Creativity
(Point to the Creativity Icon on the overhead or poster.)

Creativity is the problem solving skill. Creativity can suggest new ideas, find new ways, and invent new tools. In addition to battling the EPT's, Creativity is immensely useful in adding beauty and interest to life through art and music. Whether in arts or science, academics or mechanics, Creativity is a very valuable skill to have.

While some people seem to naturally be more creative than others, Creativity is a skill that many be learned by anyone and is needed by everyone. We tend to think about Creativity as a skill used by artists and musicians, but it is of importance to anyone who has a problem that needs to be solved. We live in a world where creative solutions to serious problems are desperately needed. The skill of Creativity will also create opportunities for you. For example, in 1948 a Swiss Mountaineer by the name of George de Menstral was hiking in the mountains. The little burs that were clinging to his clothes were irritating and annoying. But in picking them off, it occurred to him that the same principle could be used for fastening things together. Hence was born the idea for Velcor. Thousands of people before him had the irritation of burs clinging to their clothes, but he was able to see in this irritation larger possibilities. When you possess the skill of Creativity opportunities may emerge from almost anywhere. Next on the list of C skills is Communication. I'll let *(name of reader)* tell you about that skill.

Reader - Communication

(Point to the Communication Icon on the overhead or poster.)

The ability to work effectively with others is dependent on the ability to Communicate effectively. Listening and reading skills are a source of power. They give you access to knowledge and information. Speaking and writing skills give you the power to share your knowledge with others. People without effective communication skills are severely handicapped in their relationships with others. They are limited in the opportunities available to them, and are far more vulnerable to the EPT's than those who have these skills. No matter what you do in life, the ability to effectively communicate is an asset.

Perhaps the most serious deficiency most people have in communication is their listening skills. We will be placing a lot of emphasis on listening skills in our future training sessions. Next, *(name of reader)* is going to brief you on the skill of Control.

Reader - Control

(Point to the Control Icon on the overhead or poster.)

Every person is subject to two different kinds of Control—Internal Control and External Control. Agents of EPT try to influence you through External Control and cause you to lose or give up Internal Control. The stronger your ability to exercise Internal Control over your thoughts and feelings, the less likely you are to fall victim to EPT. In addition, the greater the control you have over your thoughts and feelings the greater your chances for success in achieving the things of real importance in your life.

Although control is one of the most important skills you can have, it is also one of the most difficult to acquire. It will require your best efforts over a period of time to master this skill. For example, Control is essential to self-denial. Possessit may try to convince you that must have some particular thing. But if Criticism helps you to recognize that what you want may not be good for you, Control will give you the strength to do with out it. Similarly, Control also gives you the will and determination necessary to achieve difficult goals. At another level, Control is the skill that enables you to manage anger and other emotions, thus defeating Passionata's attempts to ruin your life. So, Control is a skill you will have constant use for. The next skill is Correction. *(name of reader)*, over to you.

Reader - Correction

(Point to the Correction Icon on the overhead or poster.)

Developing the C Skills is a life time project, and the Skill of Correction is the ability to learn from your mistakes and make the adjustments necessary to continue progressing. Prevaricator would have you believe that serious mistakes can't be fixed, that you always have to live with them. But, as you might guess, this isn't true. The C skills can show you how to make changes, and Correction Skills help you do it.

Correction, for example, gives you the ability to say, "I was wrong.' and begin the process of making necessary adjustments in your beliefs and choices as appropriate. You can't imagine how important it is, this simple ability to admit that you are wrong. Far too many people make bad choices and persist in them to the bitter end because they are too proud or too afraid to admit they were wrong.

But the sad fact is that there would be fewer people in jails, fewer broken marriages, fewer people in hospitals, and fewer conflicts between family members and friends if more individuals simply had the ability to admit they were wrong, say they were sorry if necessary, and make the necessary corrections.

Correction may not likely be the most fun skill to learn, but it could prove to be one of the most beneficial skills in you ever develop.

CONTROL

CORRECTION

CURIOSITY

CONCENTRATION

COMMUNICATION

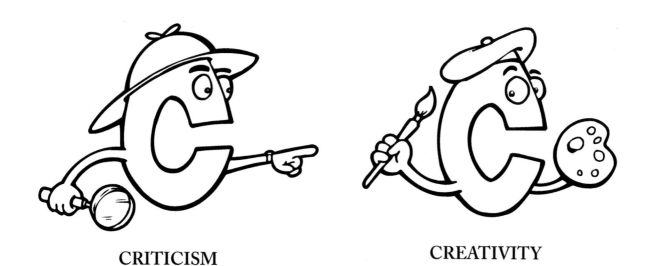

CRITICISM

CREATIVITY

THE CT SKILLS QUIZ

Fill in the name of the associated C skill in the appropriate blank and then draw a line from the skill to the icon of that skill.

You must use me to master any difficult task. Unless you can fix your attention on things long enough to master them you will be limited in what you can do.

I am the skill of _____

I help you understand the nature of things and insist that you use the standard of truth and reason to measure the worth of all things.

I am the skill of _____

You need me to work effectively with others. Without me you cannot know what they are thinking and they cannot know what you are thinking.

I am the skill of _____

I give you the ability to investigate, explore, and seek out new information. A few good questions from me can dispel myths, clarify issues, and remove confusion.

I am the skill of _____

If you make mistakes, I'm the skill that helps you fix them. Since everyone makes mistakes you can see there is a great need for me even though not everyone uses me.

I am the skill of _____

I'm the guidance skill. Not only can I help you keep from losing your temper, I can also help you in finding courage. I keep you in charge of your own thoughts and feelings.

I am the skill of _____

I'm the problem solving skill. I suggest new ideas, help you find new ways to do things and invent new tools to do them with. I also add beauty and interest to life.

I am the skill of _____

THINGS I CAN DO TO DEVELOP THE SEVEN C SKILLS

Criticism is the ability to analyze (break things into parts to observe what they are made of and see how they work), and to evaluate (measure, weigh, test, try, and compare) so as to arrive at informed judgments of value. Some things I can do to develop this skill are:

_____   _____

_____   _____

Concentration is the ability to focus my attention on things I need to know or do. It often requires me to overcome distractions. Some things I can do to develop this skill are:

_____   _____

_____   _____

Curiosity is the ability to investigate, explore, and seek out new information. It requires asking lots of questions. It involves probing, searching, and seeking. Some things I can do to develop this skill are:

_____   _____

_____   _____

Creativity is the ability to imagine, originate, invent, and design new things. It involves looking beyond the commonplace and seeing new possibilities. Some things I can do to develop this skill are:

_____   _____

_____   _____

Communication is the ability to exchange ideas, information, and knowledge through listening, speaking, reading and writing. Some things I can do to develop this skill are:

_____   _____

_____   _____

Control is the ability to govern one's thoughts and feelings. It requires self-discipline and the willingness to deny my self some things I may feel I want. Some things I can do to develop this skill are:

_____   _____

_____   _____

Correction is the ability to make necessary changes in my opinions to accommodate new information and improve results. Some things I can do to develop this skills are:

_____   _____

_____   _____

ACTIVITY 22

THE GREAT DEBATE

The debate on page 56 is a contest of reason in which the EPT (Error-Prone Thinking) team faces off against the CT (Clear Thinking) team. It is an internal contest taking place within Darcie's own thought processes. The debate provides an opportunity for students to look at a specific example of how EPT (Error-Prone Thinking) can lead us to do foolish things and how the Seven "C" skills can help a person overcome the EPT tendencies which so many of us experience.

Two different suggestions for presenting the debate are:

1. ADVANCE PREPARATION: *Photocopy the debate sheet on page 56. White out the team members of each team and then make photocopies for each student.*
    In class, explain the debate situation and introduce the members of both the EPT team and the CT team. Hand out copies of the debate and have your students, either individually or in small groups, identify the team member offering each specific argument.

2. *In class, explain the debate situation and introduce the members of both the EPT team and the CT team and then, one at a time, read each of the EPT arguments. After each EPT argument, have your students identify the EPT team member offering that argument. Then tell your students the CT team member who is responding and have them tell you what they think that "C" skill might answer.*

The Debate Situation

The teams are lined up on each side of the judges, facing one another. On one side is the EPT team, on the other is the CT team. Both teams are listening to the moderators final instructions. The situation is this: An older boy has given one of Darcie's friends a six pack of beer. Her friends are now saying, "Let's sleep outside in a tent tonight and have a party. We can drink this beer and have some fun." The two teams are to debate the question: "Shall Darcie go to the party?" The EPT team is to argue in favor of Darcie going, the CT team is against. Each team member is allowed one statement each. One member from the EPT team will speak first, and then one member from the CT team will speak next. In this manner the teams will alternate until all have spoken. At the conclusion of the debate, the judges will rule in favor of the team with the best arguments. It is time to begin. Polarizer, representing the EPT team will go first. He will be followed by Creativity.

The Team Members

Members of the EPT Team are:

Polarizer - Tells you there are only two options and it has to be one or the other.
Prevaricator - Tells lies to mislead you and make you believe things that aren't true.
Puff Benamed - Tries to group things under one name so you think they are all the same.
Puff Belarge - Exaggerates to make things seem more important to you than they really are.
Puff Belittle - Wants you to believe something is less important to you than it really is.
Puff Beblamed - Doesn't want you to take responsibility, but to pass the blame on to someone else.
Puff Prejudge - Tries to make you strongly believe in things you really know little about.

The CT Team members are:

Control - Gives you the ability to exercise physical and mental self-discipline
Communication - Gives you the ability to effectively exchange information with others
Concentration - Gives you the ability focus your attention for an extended period of time
Curiosity - Gives you the ability to investigate, explore, and seek out new information
Creativity - Gives you the ability to imagine, originate, invent, and design new things
Criticism - Gives you the ability to analyze, evaluate, and make judgments of comparative worth
Correction - Gives you the ability to revise your opinions to accommodate new information

Hindsight Questions
- What did you learn from the Great Debate?

Insight Questions
- Why does it take a conscious effort to develop the Seven "C" skills?
- Why is it sometimes difficult to focus on developing these skills?

Foresight Questions
- Why is it important to develop the seven "C" skills in your life?

ACTIVITY 23

CALL 911 FOR THE CT SKILLS

ADVANCE PREPARATION: *Prepare copies of page 57 for each student or for small group discussions. In class, either in small groups or as individuals, take each situation one at a time and identify how each C skill might be able to help the respective individual.*

Hindsight Questions
- What EPT agents were working on (Winston/Hillary/Anna)?

Insight Questions
- What is keeping (Winston/Hillary,Anna) from thinking clearly?
- Why is it a difficult thing to keep our minds free from error-prone thinking?
- Why are strong thinking skills necessary to overcome error-prone thinking?

Foresight Questions
- What kind of problems is (Winston/Hillary/Anna) headed for if he/she doesn't get his/her thinking turned around?

> **Discussion Opportunity:** Perhaps the greatest battles any of us will fight will be within our own minds, and the success or failure of these battles will depend largely on our thinking skills. The tendencies for error-prone thinking are so common and so powerful they cannot be overcome without a conscious, determined effort to do so. Character Traits: PR duty, ownership; SR self-reliance

THE GREAT DEBATE

Polarizer
Darcie if you don't go to the party, your friends won't want anything to do with you. Are you going to be one of them or not?

Prevaricator
Hey don't worry. No one will ever know. Besides beer can't hurt you.

Puff Benamed
Don't be a goodie goodie little momma's girl Darcie. If you don't do this you're chicken.

Puff Beblamed
You don't have to accept responsibility for this Darcie. Just say your friends made you do it. It is their fault you know.

Puff Belarge
But all kids do it Darcie. They just don't let on. Anyway being with your friends is more important than anything else.

Puff Belittle
Hey, it's no big deal. You're just going to drink a little beer and have a little fun. It's not like you are going to do anything stupid. What can be wrong with that?

Puff Prejudge
Hey, your friends are pretty cool. If it's good enough for them, it should be good enough for you. There's nothing to even think about.

Creativity
Darcie what do these friends need, a copy cat or someone with better ideas about how to have fun? Suggest some other options for the party like making your own movie or having a lip sync of your favorite music.

Critical Analysis
You will know even if no one else does. And if you are caught, how will you feel? More importantly, even a little alcohol can alter your judgment and cause you to do things that may be hurtful to you or others. Besides, in some people just one drink can lead to addiction.

Communication
Is being a goodie goodie a bad thing? A great test of whether this is right for you is to ask "Who am I willing to talk with about it?"

Control
Who do you want to control your life, Darcie? If you want control, you have to accept responsibility for what you do. You can't blame others for things you do. You are the one making the choice.

Concentration
Think seriously Darcie. Focus on what is being said here. Listen very carefully. Do all the kids really do it? Is being with your friends really the most important thing in your life?

Curiosity
Darcie, why is this something you have do it in secret? Why are there laws against it? How can it hurt you? What is wrong with it? What more do you need to know about alcohol and it's effect on people, especially minors.

Correction
Erase that thought. This has gone too far. You need to get out of here. You don't need to be cool. You need to be smart. Get your mind on another track and think about something that will make you a better person.

CALL 911 FOR THE CT SKILLS

Situation One

Winston was furious. No one could call him creep and get away with it. He knew where his dad kept a 22 pistol. He'd show them a thing or two.

Situation Two

Hillary was pleased. Her mother believed her story. Now she could go with her friends and not worry that her mother would come looking for her.

Situation Three

Anna was mimicking Wanda's lisp. Everyone was roaring with laughter. Everyone but Wanda that is. Wanda was trying to smile, but wasn't very successful.

Situation _____

Why is this person thinking or acting in this manner? Which EPT agents are working on him/her?

What is required of Criticism?

What must Concentration do?

How can Curiosity help?

Where does Creativity come in?

What role can Communication play?

What must Control do?

What is required of Correction?

ACTIVITY 24

BENJAMIN FRANKLIN USES THE SEVEN C SKILLS

24-1 _____ The Happiness or Real Good of Men _____

ADVANCE PREPARATION: *Photocopy the following dialogue for each student. Assign a student to practice reading each part in advance of class.*
Prior to handing out copies for each student, have the two students read the dialogue to the class (practice listening skills) and discuss. After the discussion, hand out copies to each student and have the two students reread the dialogue with the other students reading along. Discuss again.

Dialogue

Philocles: The chief faculty in man is his reason, and consequently his chief good, or that which may be justly called his good, consists not merely in action, but in reasonable action. By reasonable actions we understand those actions which are preservative of the human kind and naturally tend to produce real and unmixed happiness; and these actions, by way of distinction, we call morally good.

Horatio: You speak very clearly, Philocles; but, that no difficulty may remain on my mind, pray tell me what is the real difference between natural good and evil and moral good and evil?

Philocles: The difference lies only in this: that natural good and evil are pleasure and pain; moral good and evil are pleasure and pain produced with design and intention; for it is the intention only that makes the agent morally good or bad.

Horatio: But may not a man with a very good intention do an evil action?

Philocles: Yes; but then he errs in judgment, though his design be good. If his error is inevitable, or such, as all things considered, he could not help, he is inculpable; but if it arose through want of diligence in forming his judgments about the nature of human actions, he is immoral and culpable.

Horatio: I find, then, that in order to please ourselves rightly, or to do good to others morally, we should take great care of our opinions.

Philocles: Nothing concerns you more; for as the happiness or real good of men consists in right action, and right action cannot be produced without right opinion, it behooves us, above all things in this world, to take care that our own opinions of things be according to the nature of things. The foundation of all virtue and happiness is thinking rightly.

from *Benjamin Franklin's The Art of Virtue* P. 29-30

Hindsight Questions
- What was the difference between natural good and evil and moral good and evil?
- Why is it important for our opinions of things to be according to the nature of things?

Insight Questions
- What did Franklin mean when he said, "right action cannot be produced without right opinion?"
- What does he mean by the term, "the nature of things."

Foresight Questions:
- What can you do to take care that your opinions of things are according to the nature of things?

Discussion Opportunity: Criticism is an essential skill in helping a person arrive at an understanding of the nature of things. The nature of things is things as they really are, not as we imagine or wish them to be. If we truly understand the nature of our choices, we can anticipate what the consequences of those choices might be. If we understand the nature of things, we can recognize those actions that will produce real and unmixed happiness vs. actions that might produce temporary pleasure, but in the long run create pain and sorrow. The ability to analyze, interpret, compare, and evaluate information is essential to arriving at such understandings. Without this skill, we are highly vulnerable to error prone thinking. Character Traits: PR duty, ownership; T dependability

24-2   Which of the Seven C Skills is Franklin Using?

ADVANCE PREPARATION: *Photocopy the activity sheet on page 60 for each student.*

Explain that the activity sheet contains quotes from the writings of Benjamin Franklin. Some are from letters to friends, some are from his autobiography. Have students compete the activity sheet by circling those C skills they think Franklin is talking about in each statement and afterwards discuss their answers.

Hindsight Questions
- Which C Skills do you think Franklin was using in this statement?
- What was Franklin saying in this statement?

Insight Questions:
- Why do you think Franklin said or did that?

Foresight Questions
- How might what Franklin said or did here be helpful to you?

Discussion Opportunity: Benjamin Franklin was perhaps one of the most brilliant men to have ever lived. Yet, he did not trust his own reasoning processes. To protect himself from error-prone thinking, he deliberately developed the C skills. He did not call them the C skills or error prone thinking, but that's what he did. He developed an active curiosity that might have him flying a kite with a metal key attached to it in an attempt to attract lightening, electrocuting a turkey to see if its meat would be more tender, or trying to light a flame with a candle to a pool of water where he supposed there was some form of gas. His creativity made him a prolific inventor and problem solver. Among his many inventions were bifocal glasses. As noted in the quotes, he invested a great deal of effort into improving his communication skills and he was quick to correct himself when he found he was in the wrong. As the quotes also suggest, he knew self-control was essential to avoiding warm disputes and he actively used the skills of concentration and criticism on a regular basis. These were his safe guards to keep him from falling into error. Character Traits: PR ownership; SR self-reliance

Which of the Seven C Skills is Franklin Using?

Circle the C Skills you think Franklin used in each statement.

To a young friend, Franklin wrote, "I would advise you to read with a pen in your hand, and enter in a little book short hints of what you find." That Franklin followed his own advice can be seen in his comments on the following excerpt from an article justifying the impressing of seamen by the English navy.

JUDGE FOSTER: And as for the mariner himself, he, when taken into the service of the crown, only changeth masters for a time; his service and employment continue the very same, with this advantage, that the dangers of the sea and the enemy are not so great in the service of the crown . . . .

FRANKLIN'S COMMENTS: These are false facts. His service and employment are not the same. Under the merchant, he goes in an unarmed vessel not obliged to fight. In the king's service, he is obliged to fight. Sickness on board the king's ships is also more common. The merchants service he can quit at the end of the voyage, not the king's. Also merchant's wages are much higher.

I am persuaded you think, as I do, that he who removes a prejudice or an error from our minds contributes to their beauty, as he would do that of our faces who should clear them of a wart or wen.

By calmly discussing rather than warmly disputing, the truth is most easily obtained.

About this time I met with an odd volume of the Spectator. I thought the writing excellent, and wished, if possible to imitate it. With this view I took some of the papers, and, making short hints of the sentiment in each sentence, laid them by a few days, and then, without looking at the book, try'd to compleat the papers again, by expressing each hinted sentiment in any suitable words that came to hand. Then I compared my spectator with the original, discovered my faults, and corrected them. I took some of the tales and turned them into verse, and, after a time, when I had pretty well forgotten the prose, turned them back again. I also sometimes jumbled my collections of hints into confusion, and after some weeks endeavored to reduce them into the best order, before I began to form the full sentences and compleat the paper. This was to teach me the arrangement of thoughts.

Being in Maryland, riding with Colonel Tasker, we saw in the vale below us a whirlwind beginning in the road. . . .When it passed by us, its smaller part near the ground appeared no bigger than a common barrel; but, widening upwards, it seemed at forty or fifty feet high, to be twenty or thirty feet in diameter. The rest of the company stood looking after it; but my curiosity being stronger, I followed it, riding close by its side. As it is common opinion that a shot, fired through a water spout will break it, I tried to break this little whirlwind by striking my whip frequently through, but without effect.

BIOGRAPHY

WE HOLD THESE TRUTHS TO BE SELF-EVIDENT

In the Lincoln-Douglas debates of 1858, the central issue was more than just slavery. At the very heart of the debate was this statement from the Declaration of Independence: "All men are created equal." The debates addressed such important questions as, "Who may be considered a citizen of the United States of America?" and "What are the rights of U.S. citizenship?" Following are excerpts from speeches given by Stephen A. Douglas and Abraham Lincoln defining their respective positions regarding these important questions.

Stephen A. Douglas
Speech, July 17, 1858

Hence, you find that Mr. Lincoln and myself come to a direct issue on this whole doctrine of slavery. . . . In his Chicago speech he says [that the Declaration of Independence] includes the negroes, that they were endowed by the Almighty with the right of equality with the white man, and therefore that that right is divine—a right under the higher law; that the law of God makes them equal to the white man, and therefore that the law of the white man cannot deprive them of that right. This is Mr. Lincoln's argument. . . .

And here is the difference between us. I believe that the Declaration of Independence, in the words, "all men are created equal," was intended to allude only to the people of the United States, to men of European birth or descent, being white men, that they were created equal, and hence that Great Britain had no right to deprive them of their political and religious privileges. . . . I am not only opposed to negro equality, but I am opposed to Indian equality. I am opposed to putting the coolies, now importing into this country, on an equality with us, or putting the Chinese or any other inferior race on an equality with us. . . .The Declaration of Independence only included the white people of the U.S.

Abraham Lincoln
Speech, July 10, 1858

I have always hated slavery. . . .but I have been quiet about it until the introduction of the Nebraska bill began. . . .

We were often [told] in the course of Judge Douglas' speech last night that he believed [this government] was made for white men. . . .

Now I ask you in all soberness, if all these things, if indulged in, [and] if taught to our children, do not tend to transform this Government into a government of some other form. . . . What are these arguments? They are the arguments that kings have made for enslaving the people in all ages of the world. . . . I should like to know if taking this old Declaration of Independence, which declares that all men are equal and making exceptions to it where will it stop. If one man says it does not mean a negro, why not another say it does not mean some other man?

Speech, August 17, 1858

In [the signer's] enlightened belief, nothing stamped with the Divine image and likeness was sent into the world to be trodden on, and degraded, and imbruted by its fellows. They grasped not only the whole race of man then living, but they reached forward and seized upon the farthest posterity. They erected a beacon to guide their children and their children's children,. . . .they knew the tendency of prosperity to breed tyrants, and so they established these great self-evident truths, that when in the distant future some man, some faction, some interest, should set up the doctrine that none but rich men, or none but white men, were entitled to life, liberty and the pursuit of happiness, their posterity might look up again to the Declaration of Independence and take courage to renew the battle which their fathers began. . . .

Speech, September 11, 1858

Familiarize yourselves with the chains of bondage, and you are preparing your own limbs to wear them. Accustomed to trample on the rights of those around you, you have fit subjects of the first cunning tyrant who rises.

Hindsight Questions
- What was Douglas' position?
- What was Lincoln's position?

Insight Questions
- How would our country be different now if Douglas' way of thinking had prevailed?
- How is the phrase "all men are created equal" a protection for anyone who lives in the US?

Foresight Questions
- What does the phrase "all men are created equal" mean to you?
- How does it relate to how you treat each other at school?

Discussion Opportunity: Criticism was a skill Lincoln relied on extensively. As a result, he could see the danger of slavery, even to those who embraced it. He realized that the statement in the Declaration of Independence, "We hold these truths to be self-evident, that all men are created equal, that they are endowed by their Creator with certain unalienable Rights, that among these are Life, Liberty, and the Pursuit of Happiness—" had to be taken literally and without exception. There is a tendency in some people to want to exercise power over others. Sometimes, this tendency is manifest along racial lines, but it can be manifest along religious, political, and social lines, as well. In Lincoln's mind, for America to be free, it had to be free for every one on the same basis. This line of thinking applies not just at the national level, it applies in communities, in the work environment, and on the school yard as well. Perverter befogged Douglas and prevented him from being able to understand Lincoln's position. Puff Benamed Puff Beblamed encouraged him to name different classes of people, Puff Prejudge enabled him to class some as inferior, Puff Belarge and he was to magnify the advantages of his own race and Puff Belittle led him to minimize the worth and rights of others. A good test of Lincoln's arguments is their fairness, no matter who you are. On the other hand it is doubtful that Douglas would have liked his arguments so well if he had been black, or if he had been born Indian, Chinese, or some other race he now considered inferior. Character Traits: RO caring, fairness, citizenship

ACTIVITY 26

THE CASE OF THE MISSING STRADIVARIUS

When Inspector Numero Uno arrived at his office, he found Sergeant Tilby waiting for him.

"We had a strange occurrence last evening sir!" Tilby reported. "About nine PM our officers received a report of an elderly gentleman being accosted by a couple of thugs. The old man was playing a violin on the corner of Livingston and Cline. He had his top hat on the ground for people to put money in. Apparently, the thugs stole both the hat and the violin. When our officers arrived, the old gentleman had disappeared. According to witnesses, his music was exceptional, and his hat was full of money."

"Very interesting." replied Uno.

"But that's not all, Sir. " Sergeant Tilby continued, "About an hour later, our people responded to a report of a pawn shop robbery, just two blocks from where the old man's violin was stolen. According to officers on the scene, a Mr. Willowbe, an antique dealer who frequents pawn shops looking for good deals, was in the Three Palms Pawn Shop. He noticed a violin the owner had just taken in, but had not yet put up for sale. Mr. Willowbe immediately recognized the violin as a Stradivarius, but suspected that Mr. Goates, the pawn shop owner, had no idea of the violin's real value. Thinking to make a fortune for very little, Mr. Willowbe offered Goates a hundred dollars for the violin. Goates thought Willowbe seemed a little overanxious, and thinking he might pay more, cagily replied that the violin was surely worth more than that. Willowbe came back with an offer of two hundred and fifty dollars and the game of wits was on; Goates trying to see how much Willowbe would pay, and Willowbe trying to get the violin. When the bidding reached $5,000 Willowbe lost his temper and grabbed Goates by the neck. Goates struck back. A couple walking by, thought a robbery was in progress and called the police. When the officers arrived, the story came out.

Apparently, Goates had bought the violin from two rather rough looking characters for $50 about 9:30 PM.

The officers, piecing together the events, connected the violin with the earlier robbery of the old gentleman. In searching the neighborhood they found a top hat matching the description of the old man's hat given by witnesses. Here's the hat."

Uno looked the hat over. Inside, he saw the initials W.H. Uno closed his eyes and leaned back in his chair. He sat there for a few moments, then looked at Tilby.

At this point in the story, ask and discuss: What are some who, what, why, how, where, and when questions you think Inspector Uno might ask at this point? As students come up with the following key questions, provide the answer. Then continue the story

Key Questions:

Why did the old man who was robbed disappear?

Why has he not reported the theft of his violin and money?

What information do we have on stolen Stradivarius violins?

(All other questions.)

Key Question Answers:

He had something to hide

He had stolen the violin himself

One entrusted to Sir Winston Harcourt was stolen about 25 years ago.

Don't know or no info given yet

Continue Story:

"Go to the file on unsolved cases, and see if we have anything on missing Stradivarius violins."

"Yes sir." Tilby responded and left to see what he could find.

Shortly, Tilby returned and handed Inspector Uno an old manila folder containing several news clippings and police reports. Uno looked through the papers for a few minutes, then looked at Sergeant Tilby and said, "Look at this!"

"What do you see?" asked Tilby.

"Now I remember," Uno began, "Just about twenty-five years ago, Sir Winston Harcourt was one of the world's most famous violinists. He was invited to play at a command performance for the Queen. Because of the nature of this performance, Sir Winston was able to borrow a Stradivarius violin from the London Museum of Arts. While the violin was in his possession, Sir Winston was allegedly attacked by robbers, beaten, and the violin was stolen. Although, the circumstances of the robbery were suspect, no hard evidence could be produced linking Sir Winston with the robbery, and the Stradivarius had vanished from sight.

Because of the bad publicity, Sir Winston's popularity faded, and it appeared he lost all interest in playing publicly. Eventually he became a recluse, seeing no one, and no one seeing him. Come, Sergeant, let's go pay a call on Sir Winston Harcourt."

A half hour later, Inspector Uno and Sergeant Tilby pulled up in front of an old, run down mansion. They knocked at the door and waited. When the door opened, Inspector Uno said, "Sir Winston, we've come to return your hat."

"Come in gentlemen," Sir Winston responded, "I've been expecting you."

Sir Winston led them to a large parlor and invited them to be seated. He then said, "Did you retrieve the violin also?"

"Yes." Uno replied.

"Was it damaged?"

"No" Uno said.

"Thank goodness!" Sir Winston sounded relieved.

"The night I played for the queen," Sir Winston volunteered, "was a magical moment. I became obsessed with the violin. Nothing else was important to me but to be able to play it. That violin produced the most beautiful sounds I had ever heard. For years now, I have spent the nearly whole of every night playing the violin in the seclusion of a secret room here in my house. Eventually, I needed money. I had sold everything I owned to keep going. I thought perhaps I could play on the street and no one would recognize me. But, I guess I realized it was just a matter of time."

Hindsight Questions
- Which members of EPT influenced Sir Winston Harcourt in the choices he made?
- Which C skills did Inspector Uno use in solving this case?

Insight Questions
- Why would it have been difficult to solve this case without these skills?
- What was important to Sir. Winston Harcourt?
- What apparently was not important to Sir Winston?

Foresight Questions
- If Sir Winston had used similar C skills, how might he have avoided his problems?

Discussion Opportunity: Possessit got hold of Sir Winston Harcourt. Then Perverter blew Puff Belarge and Puff Belittle in his eyes. Under their influence, having possession of the Stradivarius became more important to Sir Winston than anything else in the world. The rights of other people, and even his own well-being were totally ignored. Only one thing mattered to him. Curiosity was the thinking skill most helpful to Inspector Uno at this time. Criticism and Concentration also helped him in asking the right questions. Character Traits: PR duty, accountability; RO caring, T honesty

BIOGRAPHY

ACTIVITY 27

I STRUGGLED TO STAY AWAKE

This biographical sketch of Charles Lindburgh is written in the first person. Have your students guess who this person is.

My confidence nearly left me as soon as the wheels of my little airplane lifted off the muddy runway, barely clearing the telephone wires in front of me. My preparations for this trip had been exhaustive. Months of planning and preparation had gone before this day. The airplane, itself was built to my specifications, and there was not a single ounce of wasted weight in the plane. I was flying solo, without either a radio or a parachute. My only provisions were five sandwiches and a quart of water, even though I knew the flight would take at least 30 hours. I told a member of my ground crew, "If I get to Paris I won't need any more. If I don't get to Paris I won't need anymore either."

I had only been in flight for a little over an hour when I reached the coast. I recorded my feelings, "Looking ahead at the unbroken horizon and limitless expanse of water, I'm struck by my arrogance in attempting such a flight. I'm giving up a continent and heading out to sea in the most fragile vehicle ever devised by man. . . .Why have I dared stake my life in the belief. . . .that I can find my way through shifting air to Europe?"

The flight was long and difficult. I struggled to stay awake and nearly lost control of the plane when I flew into an ice cloud and the wings became covered with ice. But eventually the long night ended and with it the terrible struggle to stay awake. Twenty-eight hours after take off, I saw the coast of Ireland and was again flying over land. It was night again by the time I reached Paris. Strangely, as I watched the bright lights of Paris grow closer, I regretted the flight was over. Who am I?

Hindsight Questions
- Who was this person?
- What was the most difficult part of his flight?

Insight Questions
- Why was Lindbergh willing to risk his life to fly nonstop from New York to Paris?
- How important to Lindbergh was the skill of Concentration? Why?

Foresight Questions
- Why do you think Lindbergh went to such extensive preparations for this flight?
- What can you learn from his approach to this dangerous undertaking?

Discussion Opportunity: Lindbergh fully understood the risks of this flight. He had used the skills of Curiosity and Criticism to help him identify and analyze what would be needed, both in terms of the aircraft and his own personal preparations. Creativity, Communication, and Correction had helped him make those preparations. Now it was up to Concentration and Control to get him to Paris. If they failed him, all else was for naught. Character Traits: SR self-reliance

BIOGRAPHY

ACTIVITY 28

AMONG MY DETRACTORS

A biographical sketch of Louis Pasteur is written in the first person. Have your students guess who this person is.

June 2, 1881 was perhaps one of the most dramatic days of my life. When we arrived at the property of M. Rossignol, a large crowd was already gathered. As I stepped down from the carriage, I was given a loud cheer. The results of the test were conclusive. Twenty-one of the unvaccinated sheep were already dead and two died in front of the spectators while we were standing there. The final sheep died that evening. All of the vaccinated sheep were alive and well.

Although I had entered into this public demonstration of vaccination with a high degree of confidence, I was greatly relieved. I had devoted the last several years of my life entirely to the study of microbes and the understanding of germs. I had already performed this experiment with fourteen sheep in my laboratory using the most exacting experimental methods. As a result, I had a better understanding of how diseases were spread and the principles of immunization than any other person then living. I knew that animals injected with a mild form of a disease causing germ would develop a resistance to stronger, life threatening forms of the same germ. I had done it many times. For example, I had learned that a chicken injected first with a mild cholera bacteria would almost never die when later injected with a strong cholera bacteria. On the other hand, a chicken not receiving the mild injection would nearly always die when injected with the strong bacteria. In the case of the sheep, the disease was anthrax. While the techniques for obtaining the vaccine were different for anthrax than for cholera because the microbes were different, the principles were the same. I had worked with these diseases and their causes for some time. I knew very well

their course and was absolutely certain that vaccination was the means to prevent them. Nevertheless, I was greatly relieved the test proved to be so conclusive. These methods had never before been attempted outside of my laboratory, and certainly not in field conditions. Furthermore, there were those who wished to see the experiment fail.

Among my detractors was M. Rossignol, in whose field the test took place. Rossignol was a veterinarian who refused to believe the germ theory and challenged me to a public demonstration of the immunization methods I was expounding. It was he who proposed this public test as a means of arriving at the truth, though I'm certain it was his hope the whole thing would be a great failure. In my opinion, he was not so much interested in the truth as in preserving his own reputation. He had staked much on his opposition to me and was anxious to prove to others he was right. In reality, at the time, there were more doctors and veterinarians who believed him than who believed me. So, in my mind, a great deal was on the line in agreeing to this test. But to me, the issue at stake was far more important than his or my reputation. It was how these terrible and destructive diseases might be more effectively prevented, both in animals and in humans.

At the time of this demonstration, anthrax killed thousands of sheep and cattle in France every year, with some farmers losing as much as a half of their flock at one time. After the demonstration, we were able to develop the anthrax vaccine and inoculation methods that were used to immunize over seven million cattle and sheep during the next three years. Who am I?

Hindsight Questions
- What gave Pasteur the confidence to agree to a public demonstration of his vaccination methods?

Insight Questions
- Which of the Seven C Skills do you think Pasteur had to use most in his work?

Foresight Questions
- How could greater Curiosity have saved M. Rossignol some embarrassment?

Discussion Opportunity: Pasteur required all of the C skills in his work, but perhaps he had to rely on Curiosity, Creativity, Concentration, and Criticism most frequently. M. Rossignol allowed himself to be influenced by the Puff Prejudge befogger and rather than try to understand Pasteur's findings sought to condemn them. As a result, he gave Pasteur a challenge which put both their reputation's on the line and he came up the loser. It was M. Rossignol's responsibility to understand Pasteur's germ theory before attempting to judge it. The skills of Curiosity and Criticism could have been of great help to him if he had used them. Character Traits: PR Ownership, accountability; T dependability

---

BIOGRAPHY

ACTIVITY 29

SEVERAL THOUSAND THINGS THAT WON'T WORK

A biographical sketch of Thomas Edison written in the first person. Have your students guess who this person is.

After thirteen months of ceaseless experiments, I concluded that I was simply on the wrong track. Platinum filaments could never be made to last. For the electric light bulb to be useful, we needed to find a substance that would enable the light to glow for much longer periods of time without burning out.

Then one day, almost by accident, I hit upon the idea of carbon filaments. Several more weeks of innumerable experiments and ceaseless labor passed with little success. Then on October 21, 1879 came the major break through. After two days and two nights without rest or sleep, Charles Bachelor, one of my close associates, and I were able to successfully attach a small carbonized piece of cotton thread in the bulb. When lit, it burned for 45 hours. Although it would take several more years to perfect the incandescent bulb, I now knew that we were on the right track.

During this period, one of my young assistants said to me, "Sir, it's a shame that we should have worked all these weeks without getting any results." I replied, "Results! Why, man, I have gotten a lot of results! I now know several thousand things that won't work." Who am I?

Hindsight Questions
- Who was this person?
- How long did it take Thomas Edison to invent the light bulb?

Insight Questions
- How did Curiosity help Edison in finding a proper filament for the light bulb?
- What kind of Creativity would it take to undertake a thousand different experiments?

Foresight Questions
- How do you think Curiosity and Creativity might help you solve problems in your life?

ACTIVITY 30

BIOGRAPHY

THE BEGINNINGS OF A NOBEL PRIZE

Her laboratory was a tiny bedroom hidden away from the police. Her tools were sewing needles ground into miniature scalpels and spatulas, miniature scissors obtained from an opthamologist, and tiny forceps from a watchmaker. The microscopic surgery she performed was on fertilized chicken eggs. Rita Levi-Montalcini was studying the nervous system as it developed in embryonic chicks. It was World War II and Rita lived in Italy. At that time in Italy, there was a law forbidding Jews to practice science or medicine. Rita had to work in secret to learn how the nervous system is formed and how it works.

Nightly bombing raids often forced Rita into a basement bomb shelter, where she slept with her microscope and slides to protect them from possible damage. As anti-Jewish sentiment worsened, she and her family moved to the country.

During the war, eggs became very difficult to get. Frequently Rita bicycled through the hills asking farmers for eggs, somehow finding enough to keep her research going. Working in isolation, without the opportunity of collaborating with other scientists, and and in a world that seemed to be going mad, Rita laid the foundation for her discovery of (NFG) nerve growth factor. For her discovery of NFG, Rita receive a Nobel Prize in Medicine and Physiology in 1986. The importance of these growth factors is their influence on the development of immature cells and the role they play in certain degenerative diseases that affect the central nervous system.

Of her experience in conducting these experiments in the conditions she worked under during the war, Rita later said, "It was a pure miracle that I succeeded with such primitive instrumentation. It cannot be repeated." Rita continued the work she had begun during the war, and for the next forty years continued to make important contributions to science. The Nobel Prize was just one of many important recognitions that were to come to Rita for her work.

Hindsight Questions
- How did Rita get the tools she needed for her work?

Insight Questions
- Which of the Seven C Skills do you think Rita needed for her work? Why?
- How important was Curiosity in her work?
- How important was Creativity?

Foresight Skills
- What do you think motivated Rita to keep working under these conditions?

Discussion Opportunity: Curiosity, Creativity, Concentration, and Criticism were essential skills in Rita's work. Perverter convinced her government that her work was of no value. To overcome the many obstacles she faced, she had to constantly draw on inner reserves to motivate and move her forward. Character Traits: SR self-reliance

ACTIVITY 31

GETTING TO KNOW YOU

31-1   Getting to Know Each Other

Brainstorm a list of questions that would be helpful in getting to know another person. Select the best five or ten. Once the class has settled on a list of questions, pass around a hat with each of their names on it. If anyone draws their own name, they need to put it back and draw again. After each has the name of another person, they are to interview this person by asking the questions the class prepared. After everyone has been interviewed, ask each student to report on the person they interviewed. After the activity, ask the HIF questions below.

31-2   Getting to Know Your Neighbor

Brainstorm a list of people in the community or in your area your class would like to know more about. It might be a local celebrity, an elderly person, someone who has an interesting profession, or any number of other qualifications that would make them of interest to the class. Select those the class is most interested in and brainstorm a list of questions that would be appropriate to ask them. Then, one at a time as your schedule permits, assign a class member to invite these individuals to visit your class. The student issuing the invitation should: 1) inform the invitee that members of the class want to get to know more about him or her, 2) explain the questions the class has prepared, and 3) ask the person if he or she would be willing to come? Have two or three possible dates and times in mind. After the activity, discuss the HIF questions below.

Hindsight Questions
- What did you find out about this person you did not know before?

Insight Questions
- How can a healthy curiosity help us get to know people better?
- How can an unhealthy curiosity lead us to want to know things that are none of our business?
- Which Puff befoggers often keep us from getting to know people better?

Foresight Questions
- Why is it an advantage to know others better than we generally do?

Discussion Opportunity: Being genuinely interested in other people can help us make many friendships in life. If we take time to know what's important to others we often discover new interests ourselves. Curiosity is the C skill that will help us most. Puff Prejudge and Puff Benamed Puff Beblamed will try to convince us we know all we need to know, or Puff Belittle will try to suggest it is not important to know anything about them. Character Traits: PR ownership; RO caring

---

BIOGRAPHY

ACTIVITY 32

FREDERICK DOUGLASS LEARNS TO READ AND WRITE

From *Narrative of the Life of Frederick Douglass, An American Slave* by Frederick Douglass

32-1 Learning to Read

Very soon after I went to live with Mr. and Mrs. Auld, [around the age of 8], she very kindly commenced to teach me the A, B, C. After I had learned this, she assisted me in learning to spell words of three or four letters. Just at this point of my progress, Mr. Auld found out what was going on, and at once forbade Mrs. Auld to instruct me further, telling her, among other things, that it was unlawful, as well as unsafe, to teach a slave to read. To use his own words, further, he said, "If you give a nigger an inch, he will take an ell. A nigger should know nothing but to obey his master—to do as he is told to do. Learning would spoil the best nigger in the world. Now," said he, "if you teach that nigger (speaking of myself) to read there would be no keeping him. It would forever unfit him to be a slave. He would at once become unmanageable, and of no value to his master. As to himself, it could do him no good, but a great deal of harm. It would make him discontented and unhappy." These words sank deep into my heart, stirred up sentiments within that lay slumbering, and called into existence an entirely new train of thought. It was a new and special revelation, explaining dark and mysterious things, with which my youthful understanding had struggled, but struggled in vain. I now understood what had been to me a most perplexing difficulty—to wit, the white man's power to enslave the black man. It was

a grand achievement, and I prized it greatly. From that moment, I understood the pathway from slavery to freedom. It was just what I wanted, and I got it at a time when I the least expected it.

. . . .From this time I was most narrowly watched. If I was in a separate room any considerable length of time, I was sure to be suspected of having a book, and was at once called to give an account of myself. All this, however, was too late. The first step had been taken. Mistress, in teaching me the alphabet, had given me the inch, and no precaution could keep me from taking the ell.

The plan which I adopted, and the one by which I was most successful, was that of making friends of all the little white boys whom I met in the street. As many of these as I could, I converted into teachers. With their kindly aid, I finally succeeded in learning to read. When I was sent of errands, I always took my book with me, and by going one part of my errand quickly, I found time to get a lesson before my return. I used also to carry bread with me, enough of which was always in the house, to which I was always welcome; for I was much better off in this regard than many of the poor white children in our neighborhood. This bread I used to bestow upon the hungry little urchins, who, in return, would give me that more valuable bread of knowledge. . . .

Hindsight Questions
- How did Frederick Douglass learn to read? How old was he?

Insight Questions
- What was required of Frederick as a person to make this effort? Which C Skills did he use?

Foresight Questions?
- What would have happened to Frederick if he had not made the effort to learn how to read?

32-2 Learning to Write

The idea of how I might learn to write was suggested to me [around the age of twelve] by being in Durgin and Bailey's ship-yard, and frequently seeing the ship carpenters, after hewing, and getting a piece of timber ready for use, write on the timber the name of that part of the ship for which it was intended. When a piece of timber was intended for the larboard side, it would be marked "L." When a piece was for the starboard side, it would be marked "S." A piece for the larboard side forward, would be marked "L.F." When a piece was for starboard side forward, it would be marked "S.F." For larboard aft, it would be marked "L.A." For starboard aft, it would be marked "S.A." I soon learned the names of these letters, and for what they were intended when placed upon a piece of timber in the ship-yard. I immediately commenced copying them, and in a short time was able to make the four letters named. After that, when I met with a boy who I knew could write, I would tell him I could write as well as he. The next word would be, "I don't believe you. Let me see you try it." I would then make the letters which I had been so fortunate as

to learn, and ask him to beat that. In this way I got a good many lessons in writing, which it is quite possible I should never have gotten in any other way. During this time my copy book was the board fence, brick wall, and pavement; my pen and ink was a lump of chalk. With these I learned mainly how to write. I then commenced and continued copying the Italics in Webster's Spelling Book, until I could make them all without looking on the book. By this time, my little Master Thomas had gone to school, and learned how to write, and had written over a number of copy books. These had been brought home, and shown to some of our neighbors, and then laid aside. My mistress used to go to class meeting at the Wilk Street meetinghouse every Monday afternoon, and leave me to take care of the house. When left thus, I used to spend the time in writing in the spaces left in Master Thomas's copy book, copying what he had written. I continued to do this until I could write in a hand very similar to that of Master Thomas. Thus, after a long, tedious effort for years, I finally succeeded in learning how to write.

Hindsight Questions
- How did Frederick Douglass learn to write? How old was he? How long did it take?

Insight Questions
- What was required of Frederick as a person to make this effort? Which C Skills did he use?

Foresight Questions?
- What would have happened to Frederick if he had not made the effort to learn how to write?

Discussion Opportunity: Frederick Douglass is a perfect example of Creative problem solving. Frederick had no support system, no one to encourage him or help him except as he enlisted them. But, he recognized that if he wanted to break free from his condition, he had to learn to read and write or he would forever be a slave—if not a slave to someone else, a slave to his own ignorance. Knowledge was to be his passport to freedom. He was surrounded by people who were enveloped with the Puff Prejudge befogger, but he refused to accept their judgment of him. Using a great deal of creativity and initiative, he found the resources to learn how to read and write, resources many people wouldn't even recognize. Eventually, Frederick did gain his freedom and became a powerful and eloquent opponent of slavery, both as a speaker and a writer. He was a key figure in rallying public opinion, both in the North and in Europe against slavery prior to and during he civil war. Character Traits: PR ownership; SR self-reliance; RO caring, fairness, citizenship

ACTIVITY 33

ZOE BECOMES AN ATHLETE

A biographical sketch of Zoe Koplowitz

There was nothing about Zoe to suggest she would, or even could, become an athlete of any kind. She was thirty-nine years old and more than sixty pounds overweight. More seriously, she could barely walk, even with crutches. Seventeen years earlier Zoe had been struck with multiple sclerosis, a disease that attacks the central nervous system, damages nerve endings, and blocks the transmission of information from the brain to other parts of the body. Zoe had great difficulty telling her legs and feet to move because the nerve transmission lines were damaged.

So how did Zoe become an athlete? And what kind of an athlete is she? Zoe Koplowitz is a marathon runner who gained fame in running the New York Marathon in twenty-one hours and thirty-five minutes. As a symbol of her speed, she carries a stuffed animal, "Flash the Miracle Racing Turtle" around her neck.

If you're asking "What makes an athlete out of a person who takes over twenty-one hours to run a marathon?" Then also ask, "What does it take to run for over twenty-one hours without stopping?" The best women marathon runners complete the race in two and one half hours. Zoe's body is working at the same level of exertion as their bodies, only she has to do it for ten times longer.

Zoe's story is simple. She had made her peace with MS and, with a partner, ran her own trucking business. She was a cheerful person, but thinking that she was limited by her condition, Zoe simply didn't do many of the things she would have liked to. One day in 1988, Zoe nearly choked to death while swallowing a vitamin C pill. She regained consciousness only after her business partner executed a Heimlich maneuver

to get the pill out. Zoe was insulted to think that she almost died from choking on a pill after all those years of living with MS. She decided it was time to reclaim the quality of life she had surrendered to her disease. The way to do it, she decided, was to do the most outrageous thing she could think of, run a marathon. For someone who could hardly walk and had to drag her left leg, this was indeed an outrageous ambition.

Zoe learned about and enrolled in the Achilles Track Club, a club for disabled runners. She also took martial arts and African dance classes to improve her movement and balance. Her first marathon was in 1988. By the time she completed the race, except for the few friends who had run with her, everyone else had long since gone home. They had to call their time in to the marathon committee the next day. During the long hours, their run had taken them past drug dealers and into some of the most dangerous parts of New York City after dark. At one point they even had a gun pulled on them. But when the gunman saw the marathon numbers pinned on them, he just shook his head. Zoe and her friends just kept on running, reaching the finish line in the wee hours of the morning.

In 1990, largely as a result of Zoe's inspiration, nearly one hundred disabled runners finished the New York Marathon. Among these runners was a Polish woman who ran on two artificial legs and an American man with cerebral palsy who pushed his wheel chair backward with his feet, and of course Zoe. This was her third marathon, and yes, she still was the last one to finish. But of all the runners, perhaps Zoe had more to savor in her accomplishment than any other runner in the race.

Hindsight Questions
- What experience convinced Zoe she needed to make some changes in her life?
- What changes did she decide to make?

Insight Questions
- What was required of Zoe physically, mentally, and emotionally to make these changes?

Foresight Questions
- How did making these changes improve Zoe's life?

> **Discussion Opportunity:** The story of Zoe is an excellent example of using the skills of Control and Correction together. The fact is that Correction nearly always requires a high degree of Internal Control to make the necessary changes. In her case, Zoe's body was exercising a form of external control over the the quality of her life. But she realized she was more than her body alone, and chose to make some changes. There were some things she couldn't change, but there were some things she could. Making these changes, however was not easy. It required a tremendous amount of effort and work, which in turn required a high level of commitment and determination. It required her to take control of both her body and mind to achieve her goal of running a marathon. In doing so she gained tremendous confidence and trust in her own capabilities and in her own worth as a person. Character Traits: PR duty, ownership, accountability; SR self-reliance

ACTIVITY 34

HELEN KELLER QUIZ

NOTE: *This activity is to be used in connection with the story of Helen Keller on page 79*

ADVANCE PREPARATION: *Prepare copies of Helen Keller Quiz on page 81.*

Introduce this activity by explaining that you are going to work on listening skills by reading an experience from the life of Helen Keller and then having them complete a quiz after hearing it. Read the story and pass out the quiz. You will note that the quiz gives explicit instructions to read all of the questions before answering any of the questions. The last question is actually a statement instructing them to turn over their paper without answering any of the questions. After reading the story, pass out the quiz and let them get started on it. If your class is typical, most, if not all, will not follow the instructions at the top of the page and will start writing answers to the questions.

Hindsight Questions
- How many went ahead and started the quiz without reading the instructions?

Insight Questions
- (To those who did) Why?
- Which C Skills could have helped you? How?

Foresight Questions
- What are the disadvantages of not knowing the instructions before undertaking a task?

BIOGRAPHY

ACTIVITY 35

OBEDIENCE IS THE GATEWAY

A biographical sketch of Anne Sullivan written in first person. Have your students guess who this person is.

I was born in 1866, the same year Jesse and Frank James organized their band of outlaws. Mostly I am known for my work with a wonderful woman who became an example of what a person with serious handicaps can do. Her name was Helen Keller. When Helen was a small child she contracted a disease which left her both blind and deaf. It was through Dr. Alexander Graham Bell, that I was invited by Helen's father to come and work with her.

When I first met Helen, her situation was indeed pitiful. But, her parents made it worse by pampering her. When I arrived, she was very spoiled. She would get what she wanted by throwing tantrums and behaving in the most unruly manner. She was rude, temperamental, demanding, and hopelessly lost in a world in which there was neither sight nor sound.

I could understand her suffering, but the more I thought about it, the more certain I became that obedience is the gateway through which knowledge, yes, and love too, enters the mind of a child. I determined that Helen must learn to depend upon me and obey me before I could make any headway in teaching her. Accordingly, I approached Captain and Mrs. Keller and obtained permission for Helen and I to live apart from the rest of the family, in a little garden house on the estate that wasn't being used. They were reluctant at first, but I was insistent. It was the only way I could get her to cooperate with me.

For the first few days, it was a contest of wills, but as I wrote to a friend, "fortunately for us both, I am a little stronger, and quite as obstinate." In the end, Helen responded to what I was trying to teach her. Eventually, we became devoted friends. By the time I died, Helen had graduated with honors from Radcliff college, written a book, and had traveled widely bringing a message of hope and encouragement to handicapped people everywhere. Who am I?

Hindsight Questions
- Who is this person?
- What were some Corrections Helen needed to make in her life?

Insight Questions
- In what way is obedience a gateway for knowledge and love to enter the mind of a child?
- When may obedience be considered a form of internal control?

Foresight Questions
- What would have happened if Anne Sullivan had not come into Helen Keller's life?

Discussion Opportunity: What would have happened to Helen if Anne Sullivan had not been persistent and patient? What would have happened to Helen if she had refused to make corrections in her life? Persistence, patience, and the ability to make corrections are all important qualities we need to develop. None one of us can ever be wholly successful without them. But, these are qualities only caring people can ever possess. Character Traits: SR persistence, patience; RO caring

BIOGRAPHY

ACTIVITY 36

EVERYTHING HAS A NAME!

From *Helen Keller, The Story of My Life* by Helen Keller

The most important day I remember in all my life is the one on which my teacher, Anne Mannsfield Sullivan, came to me. I am filled with wonder when I consider the immeasurable contrasts between the two lives which it connects. It was the third of March 1887, three months before I was seven years old.

On the afternoon of that eventful day, I stood on the porch, dumb, expectant. I guessed vaguely from my mother's signs and from the hurrying to and fro in the house that something unusual was about to happen, so I went to the door and waited on the steps. The afternoon sun penetrated the mass of honey suckle that covered the porch, and fell on my upturned face. My fingers lingered almost unconsciously on the familiar leaves and blossoms which had just come forth to greet the sweet southern spring. I did not know what the future held of marvel or surprise for me. Anger and bitterness had preyed upon me continually for weeks and a deep languor had succeeded this passionate struggle. . . .

I felt approaching footsteps. I stretched out my hand as I supposed to my mother. Some one took it, and I was caught up and held close in the arms of her who had come to reveal all things to me, and, more [than all else], to love me.

The morning after my teacher came she led me into her room and gave me a doll. The little blind children at the Perkins Institution had sent it and Laura Bridgman had dressed it; but I did not know this until afterward. When I had played with it a little while, Miss Sullivan slowly spelled into my hand the word "d-o-l-l." I was at once interested in this finger play and tried to imitate it. When I finally succeeded in making the letters correctly I was flushed with childish pleasure and

pride. Running downstairs to my mother I held up my hand and made the letters for doll. I did not know that I was spelling a word or that words existed; I was simply making my fingers go in monkey-like imitation. In the days that followed I learned to spell in this uncomprehending way a great many words, among them pin, hat, cup and a few verbs like sit, stand and walk. But my teacher had been with me several weeks before I understood that everything has a name.

One day, while I was playing with my new doll, Miss Sullivan put my rag doll in my lap also, spelled "d-o-l-l" and tried to make me understand that "d-o-l-l" applied to both. Earlier in the day we had had a tussle over the words m-u-g" and "w-a-t-e-r." Miss Sullivan had tried to impress it upon me that "m-u-g" is mug and that "w-a-t-e-r" is water, but I persisted in confounding the two. In despair she had dropped the subject for the time, only to renew it at the first opportunity.

I became impatient at her repeated attempts and, seizing the new doll, I dashed it upon the floor. I was keenly delighted when I felt the fragments of the broken doll at my feet. Neither sorrow nor regret followed my passionate outburst. I had not loved the doll. In the still, dark world in which I lived there was no strong sentiment or tenderness. I felt my teacher sweep the fragments to one side of the hearth, and I had a sense of satisfaction that the cause of my discomfort was removed. She brought my hat, and I knew I was going out into the warm sunshine. This thought, if a wordless sensation may be called a thought, made me hop and skip with pleasure.

We walked down the path to the well-house, attracted by the fragrance of the honeysuckle with which it was covered. Some one was drawing water and my teacher placed my hand under the spout. As the cool stream gushed over one hand she spelled into the other the word water, first slowly, then rapidly. I stood still, my whole attention fixed upon the motions of her fingers.

Suddenly, I felt a misty consciousness as of something forgotten—a thrill of returning thought; and somehow the mystery of language was revealed to me. I knew then that "w-a-t-e-r" meant the wonderful cool something that was flowing over my hand. That living word awakened my soul, gave it light, hope, joy, set it free! There were barriers still, it is true, but barriers that could in time be swept away.

I left the well-house eager to learn. Everything had a name, and each name gave birth to a new thought. As we returned to the house every object which I touched seemed to quiver with life. That was because I saw everything with the strange new sight that had come to me. On entering the door I remembered the doll I had broken. I felt my way to the hearth and picked up the pieces. I tried vainly to put them together. Then my eyes filled with tears; for I realized what I had done, and for the first time I felt repentance and sorrow.

Hindsight Questions
- How was Helen feeling before Anne came?
- How did Helen feel when she discovered everything has a name?
- What skill was Anne teaching Helen?

Insight Questions
- How difficult would it be to think if you couldn't give things a name?
- How important are words in communicating with others?
- How important are words in communicating with yourself?

Foresight Questions
- Why is it important to develop a good understanding of words and their meanings?
- What happens when people are careless with their use of language?

Discussion Opportunity: An early childhood disease took away Helen Keller's ability to see and hear. Her only connection with the world in which she lived was through touch, taste, and smell. She and her parents struggled to find ways to communicate with each other, but with little success until Anne Sullivan came into their lives. They were very limited in ways to express feelings or share ideas with each other. Helen was even limited in her ability to think and form ideas until she could find a way to give names to things and to learn to use words to describe her thoughts and feelings. Many people under value the importance of language in their lives. Although, Helen's situation is an extreme example, most of us have occasions in which we have difficulty expressing our thoughts, or explaining how we feel about something. We also have occasions when we fail to understand what someone else is trying to tell us. The ability to effectively communicate with others is one of the most important skills we can possess. Character Traits: PR duty, ownership; SR self-understanding, self-reliance; RO caring, citizenship

---

HELEN KELLER QUIZ

Please read all questions on the quiz before writing your answers.

True or False

_____ 1) The most important day in Helen's life was the day Anne Sullivan came to teach her.

_____ 2) Before Anne Sullivan came, Helen didn't even know words existed.

_____ 3) Helen was sorry when she accidentally broke her doll.

_____ 4) When Helen first learned to spell the word d-o-l-l with her fingers, she knew what the word doll meant.

_____ 5) The most important day in Helen's life was the day she learned what the word w-a-t-e-r meant.

_____ 6) Helen felt a sense of satisfaction when she felt her teacher sweep up the doll fragments after she had broken it.

_____ 7) When Helen learned that w-a-t-e-r was the name of that "wonderful cool something" flowing over her hand, she felt her soul was awakened and set free.

_____ 8) When Helen left the well-house she felt she now knew everything she needed to know and had no desire to learn anything more.

_____ 9) The first time Helen felt sorrow and repentance was when she could not put her doll back together.

_____ 10) Turn over the quiz and do not write any answers on this paper.

BIOGRAPHY

ACTIVITY 37

KAREN'S JOURNAL

The Journal entries are from the book *Karen's Test*, copyright 1989, by Gladys Clark Farmer
Permission by Deseret Book Publishing, Salt Lake City

Karen Backman died on April 14, 1987, just seven days after her 23rd birthday. A rare form of the illness neurofibromatosis claimed her life after seven years of near-constant pain and suffering. Neurofibromatosis is a genetic disorder that causes the growth of benign tumors on the body.

In Karen's case, the disease turned inward, creating large growths in her body, primarily on her brain and in her spinal column. Nerves pinched by the tumors no longer functioned properly, resulting in significantly decreased vision and near total deafness. Her vocal cords became paralyzed so she could hardly speak.

It became impossible for her to eat normally so she had to be fed through a tube implanted in her stomach. During a surgery to remove a tumor on her brain, nerves were severed that caused the right corner of her mouth to droop, making it impossible for her to smile.

Suffering with nausea, headaches, and back pains most of this period, and struggling with the handicaps described above, Karen graduated from high school with a 3.9 grade average and was a Junior in college at the time of her death.

Of particular interest is a journal Karen maintained of her thoughts, feelings, and experiences in attempting to deal with the problems created by her illness.

Entries from Karen's Journal

"Tonight we had a school dance. Of course no boys asked me so I had a boring, sad, horrible night with a little cold to go along. I sure felt bad about not being asked. It wasn't bugging me till some boys started to tease me, 'Karen, want to dance? Go with a gorilla then,' and stuff like that. . . . .Then to top it off one of my friends that's about as popular as me got asked out for pizza after. It was awful. I guess I'll have to be boy crazy inside and not out. I know its my dumb braces and thick glasses, and that makes me mad because I can't help it."

". . . .I'm a blind girl in this play and I was thinking after the play, I really am grateful I'm not blind. I have it a lot worse than most kids I know but I don't care at all. I'm so grateful I can see. Other kids take vision for granted but not me . . .I guess I take hearing and smelling for granted because I don't have any defects there. . ."

"I still feel awful about my voice. I always feel so dumb. Last week a kid at school asked me why I sounded like a muppet, and lots of people, especially the neighbors, are always teasing me about it. I wish people would understand there is nothing I can do about it. . ."

"What boy will ever look at me?. . . .How could I ever get married? I'll never date. No boy wants to go out with a girl who looks like a freak."

"Dr. Gaufin just called. Here's the news: The ringing in my deaf ear is caused by disturbed nerves in the brain stem (where the tumor was) and there is nothing they can ever do about it. I've just got to learn to live with it. . .so it looks like I'll be getting head pains and aches and living on pain killers the rest of my life. But worst of all, they said the tumor is growing and heading for my ear so that is why my hearing is going and it's just going to keep getting gradually worse until I go deaf! I'm going deaf. How can I face that? I guess I have to and it's hard to imagine right now, but I just pray I have my hearing long enough to normally graduate from high school. I just think of all the things I won't be able to do when I'm deaf. It's terrible."

"I figured out what is wrong with me. I don't know HOW to be deaf. I'm scared stiff to be around people and panic when they talk to me and I can't hear. I think I'll like school better once people know I'm deaf and I've adjusted to it. There is a lot I need to learn."

"I may have a disease that can cause me A LOT of problems through life, but I'm not going to let it stop me. I don't care what happens to me physically, I'm not going to be a nobody. I don't care what kind of an invalid I turn out to be, I'm still going to make something out of my life. When I get up to heaven I'm going to be able to look down and say, I did it. I made life worthwhile. I'm not going to have blown my only chance.

". . . I just don't see the use in living any other way, because if you don't make something of your life, no matter what your situation, then you blew your chance on earth, and it was a waste."

Hindsight Questions
- How did Karen's attitude evolve as the seriousness of her condition became more apparent to her?
- What were some of Karen's concerns?
- What did Karen seem to worry about most?

Insight Questions
- How might you feel if you were in her situation?
- How did Karen communicate with herself during this process?
- How did Karen's journal help her resolve to make something of her life no matter what her circumstances were?

Foresight Questions
- Why is it necessary to take control of your self-talk when facing difficult situations?

Discussion Questions: Karen's journal entries are examples of one form of self-talk. Karen was in need of making frequent Corrections in her thinking if she was not to be wholly Controlled by her body and by what others said to and about her. She had to constantly battle Error-Prone Thinking, the tendency to minimize her own worth as a person, the inclination to place too much value on what others think, and the natural desire to want things to be different. By expressing her feelings and problems in a formal manner in her journal, Karen was better able to understand her feelings and deal with them in a positive manner. As Karen came to recognize that her disease would not go away, she made the courageous determination to make something of her life, no matter what happened to her. It took a great deal of internal control and nearly constant Corrections for Karen to keep from giving in to her illness. Character Traits: PR ownership; SR self-understanding, self-reliance; RO caring, fairness

---

ACTIVITY 38

SCROOGE REVISITS FEZZIWIG

Adapted from *A Christmas Carol* by Charles Dickens

Oh! but he was a tight fisted hand at the grindstone. Scrooge! a squeezing, wrenching, grasping, scraping, clutching, covetous old sinner! Hard and sharp as flint, from which no steel had ever struck a generous fire, secret, and self contained, and solitary as an oyster. The cold within him froze his old features, nipped his pointed nose, shriveled his cheek, stiffened his gait, made his eyes red, his thin lips blue, and spoke out shrewdly in his grating voice.

Nobody ever stopped him in the street to say, with gladsome looks, "My dear Scrooge, how are you? When will you come see me?" No beggars implored him to bestow a trifle, no children asked of him the time, no man or woman ever once in all his life inquired the way to such and such a place, of Scrooge. Even blind men's dogs seemed to know and shun him.

Now, it so happened that one fateful Christmas eve this fearsome old skinflint was visited by the ghost of his deceased business partner, Jacob Marley, and by other spirits too. I know it's hard to believe, but its true! And, what a change it made in the old miser's life.

This Christmas eve began much as any other. Scrooge, in a foul mood, sat busy in his counting-house. It was a cold, bleak, wintery day. The door to Scrooge's counting-house was open so that he might keep his eye upon his clerk, who, in a dismal little cell, was copying letters.

"A merry Christmas, uncle! God save you!" cried a cheerful voice. It was the voice of Scrooge's nephew, who came upon him so quickly that it surprised him.

"Bah!" said Scrooge, "Humbug!"

"Christmas a humbug, uncle?" said Scrooge's nephew. "You don't mean that, I am sure."

"I do," said Scrooge. "Merry Christmas! What right have you to be merry? What reason have you to be merry? You're poor enough."

"Come, then," returned the nephew, gaily. "What right have you to be dismal? What right have you to be morose? You're rich enough."

Scrooge, having no better answer ready on the spur of the moment, said, "Bah!" again; and followed it up with another "Humbug!"

Scrooge's nephew invited his uncle to Christmas dinner, but Scrooge turned him down in the most, well, I shan't tell you what he said. During the afternoon, Scrooge also turned down an invitation to contribute to a fund for the poor and destitute. That conversation did not go well either. When time came to close for the day, Scrooge sent his clerk home with complaints about having to give him Christmas day off and strict instructions to be at work extra early the day following Christmas. With that, Scrooge returned to his own home, a dark and gloomy place lit only by candles and a small fire.

Scrooge had just prepared himself for bed when he was visited by the ghost of Jacob Marley, his former business partner. Marley was dressed as usual in a waist coat, tights, and boots, but he now had a chain clasped about his waist, and wound around him like a tail. Scrooge noticed it was made of cash-boxes, keys, padlocks, ledgers, deeds, and heavy purses wrought in steel.

Marley explained that he was forced to wear the chain he had forged in life. Marley described the misery of his existence and warned Scrooge of what he too might face, if he did not change his ways. He then informed Scrooge that he would soon be visited by the spirit of Christmas Past.

Scrooge was musing on Marley's visit and wondering whether it was something he ate, when a sudden breeze seemed to enter the room, though his windows were closed, and his curtains began to mysteriously move about. Apprehensive and somewhat frightened, Scrooge was confronted by a strange apparition who introduced himself as the Spirit of Christmas Past. He informed Scrooge that was he was going to be taken taken back to a time and place he had long since forgotten, back to the place of his first apprenticeship. As they traveled through space and time, Scrooge began to feel a surge of excitement as he recognized many of the places of his youth and to recollect this most happy period of his life.

They entered a room, as familiar to Scrooge as the back of his hand.

"Why, it's old Fezziwig! Bless his heart!" Scrooge exclaimed. Scrooge then watched as Fezziwig said to his two apprentices, "Yo ho, my boys!" said Fezziwig. No more work to night. Christmas Eve, Dick. Christmas Eve, Ebenezer." Quick as a wink the boys had the work area cleared and in came the baker, the house-maid with her cousin, and many others. In came the fiddler with his music and mountains of food. It was time for dancing and feasting. As Scrooge watched this scene from his past, fond memories flooded his mind.

As the scene passed before him, he saw the two apprentices pour out their hearts in praise to Fezziwig. The Spirit said, "Fezziwig has spent but a few pounds, is that so much that he deserves all this praise?"

Rather heatedly, and quite out of character with his present self, Scrooge replied, "It wasn't that, Spirit. He had the power to make us happy or unhappy, to make our service light or burdensome, a pleasure or a toil. In his power lay the ability to do things, in words and looks, and in things so insignificant it is impossible to count them, yet the happiness it gave us was quite as great as if it had cost a fortune."

As soon as he said it, Scrooge immediately thought of his own clerk with a twinge of remorse. But, this was to be just one of many experiences that night which would make of Scrooge, a much different man.

Hindsight Questions
- What kind of a person is Scrooge at this stage of life?
- What were Scrooge's feelings for Fezziwig?
- What did the visit of the Spirit of Christmas Past remind Scrooge of?

Insight Questions
- What did Scrooge mean when he said Fezziwig had the power to make them happy or unhappy?
- What gave Fezziwig that power?
- How did Fezziwig use that power?
- How do you suppose this experience began to change Scrooge?

Foresight Questions
- What would Scrooge's life be like if he does not change?
- How will it be different if he does change?

Discussion Opportunity: A visit to his past reminded Scrooge what it was like to be happy and helped him realize that he had it in his power to help others be happy. Now he was in the position of Fezziwig. For the first time, Scrooge was confronted with a realization that the man he was was quite different from the man he wanted to be. As a result he began to make some important corrections in his life. In turn he became a much happier person and used his wealth and influence to help others be happy as well. Think what might have happened had he not been willing to make the change. Character Traits: PR ownership, RO caring,

---

ACTIVITY 39

BUT, YOU FORGOT THE CANDLESTICKS

Adapted from *Les Miserables* by Victor Hugo

Frightened, Madame Maglorie jumped. It was the violent knock at the door that did it.

"Come in." said the Bishop. Monseigneur Bienvenu was the village priest, a man known for his kindness and generosity to those in need.

The door opened quickly and in stepped a large fierce looking man. Too frightened to even scream, she knew this was the man the villagers had been talking about. The bishop looked upon him with a tranquil eye.

Glancing quickly from one to the other, then back to the bishop, the man spoke in a loud voice,

"See here! My name is Jean Valjean. I am a convict. I have been nineteen years in the galleys. Four days ago I was set free. Today I have walked twelve leagues. This evening I went to an inn, but they turned me away because of my yellow passport."

With that he pulled from his pocket a yellow piece of paper. It read, "Jean Valjean, a liberated convict. Nineteen years in the galleys, five for burglary, fourteen for attempted escape. This man is very dangerous."

"I showed this to the mayor as required. I went to another inn. They said get out! I went to another. It was the same. I went to the prison, they would not let me in. I crept into a dog kennel and the dog bit me. I thought I would sleep in the fields, but it is cold and raining. A woman saw me in the streets. She told me to knock here. I have money. I can pay. I want some food and a place to sleep. Is this an inn? Can you give it to me? I am so hungry."

"Madame Maglorie," said the bishop, "put on another plate."

A look of unbelief came over the man, followed by a a growing smile as he slowly understood.

"You are a good man, a humane man. I beg your pardon. You are an innkeeper aren't you?"

"I am a priest who lives here." said the bishop.

"A good priest is a good thing." the man said, "Then you don't want me to pay you?"

"No!" replied the bishop, "You can keep your money. How much do you have?"

"One hundred and nine francs and fifteen sous."

"And how long did it take you to earn that?"

"Nineteen years."

"Nineteen years?" sighed the bishop.

The table was quickly set and dinner, such as it was, was soon on the table. It quickly became evident to the man that the bishop was a very poor man himself. The meal consisted of a thin soup with a little bread and cheese. In reality this was the usual fare for the bishop's household. Whatever wealth the bishop once had, and what ever had since come into his possession, he had given to the poor. The only indulgence he allowed himself was the fine silver plates on which the food was served. To brighten the occasion for their guest, the bishop had placed on the table two silver candlesticks, the plates and candlesticks representing the only wealth the bishop might still claim.

When time came for bed, Valjean noticed where Madam Maglorie stored the silver plates. Exhausted, he simply fell on the bed he was given and immediately fell asleep.

It was about three in the morning when he awoke, unable to sleep any longer. All he could think of was the silver plates which he guessed would bring him over two-hundred francs if he took them. Acting on his thoughts, he arose, silently crept to the cabinet where the plates were stored, removed them and quickly fled the house.

Upon learning their guest had stolen the silver plates, the bishop merely said, "Madame Maglorie, perhaps I have for a long time wrongly withheld this silver. It belongs to the poor, and was not this a poor man?"

That evening, there was a knock at the door.

"Come in." said the bishop.

The door opened and on the door step were four men, three gendarmes, the fourth a prisoner. Recognizing the prisoner as his guest of the previous evening, the good bishop stepped forward,

"Ah, there you are." he said, "I am glad to see you. But why did you not take the candle sticks. I gave them to you as well and they are worth at least two hundred francs."

"Then Monseigneur, what this man said was true? You did give him the silver plates?"

"Yes, my good man, and the candlesticks as well. He has great need for them you see."

At this, the gendarmes released Valjean who stated to shrink away.

"My friend," the bishop said, "do not forget your candlesticks."

Quickly, he stepped to the fireplace, removed the two silver candlesticks from the mantelpiece, and took them to Valjean. Handing them to the surprised man, the bishop said,

"Forget not, never forget, you have promised me you will use this sliver to become an honest man."

As Valjean left the bishops house and resumed his journey, he was more confused than clear about what had happened to him. That the savagery had not completely left him was evident when stole forty sous from a young boy shortly after. But as mean and low as this act was, it had one redeeming feature. It brought Valjean face to face with the man he had become and realize it was not the man he wanted to be.

For the first time in many years, he fell to the ground and wept. And as he wept, it seemed to wash from his soul all of the bitterness and hatred that had accumulated during his harsh years of imprisonment. At that point Valjean resolved to be an honest man and use the money from the silver to do all the good he could.

On entering the city of his destination, Valjean found a house on fire, and at the risk of his own life, saved two children who proved to be the children of the captain of the gendarmerie. In the gratitude and confusion of the moment the Captain did not think to ask for his passport and, from that time on, Valjean was known by the name of Monsieur Madeline.

In twelve short years Monsieur Madeline, our Jean Valjean, rose to become a highly prosperous manufacturer, known for his kindness and generosity. His ingenuity in business was only excelled by the generosity of his pocket. Indeed, any who applied to him for employment were hired. His only condition for employment being the following instructions, "Be an honest man." or, "Be an honest woman."

Hindsight Questions
- What kind of a person was Jean Valjean before he met the priest?
- What was he like after?

Insight Questions
- What caused Jean Valjean to change?
- How did he see the world differently after he changed?

Foresight Questions
- Why did he instruct his employees to be honest?
- Why is it helpful from time to time to ask yourself, "What kind of person do I want to be?" and "What to I need to do to become that kind of person?"

> **Discussion Opportunity:** Perverter, Possessit, and Passionata nearly destroyed this poor man. But a good priest who took his calling seriously, Communicated through his kindness and generosity the benefits of being honest. Criticism helped Valjean understand and Control helped him make the necessary Corrections in his life. Character Traits: PR right, ownership, accountability; SR self-understanding; RO caring, citizenship; T honesty

ACTIVITY 40

INTERNAL VERSUS EXTERNAL CONTROL

39-1) *Brainstorm a list of ways in which people try to control their environment. Then ask and discuss why people feel a need to control their environment. Next brainstorm a list of ways in which people try to control others. Ask and discuss why people feel a need to control others. Finally, brainstorm a list of ways in which people may control themselves. Ask and discuss why people have a need to control themselves. Discuss the HIF questions below.*

39-2) *Following are two quotes. Assign your students to write a one page paper on the meaning of either one or both. Afterwards, discuss the HIF questions below.*

> "Only a virtuous people are capable of freedom. As nations become corrupt and vicious, they have more need of masters."
> Benjamin Franklin

> "Society cannot exist unless a controlling power upon the will and appetite is placed somewhere; and the less of it there is within, the more there must be without. It is ordained in the eternal constitution of things, that men of intemperate minds cannot be free. Their passions forge their fetters."
> Edmund Burke

Hindsight Questions
- What is the difference between internal control and external control?

Insight Questions
- What types of external control are people subject to?
- How are people who do not have internal control subject to external control?
- Why must there be a controlling power upon the will and appetite of individuals?

Foresight Questions
- What are some of the problems of being controlled by external influences?
- Why is it to your advantage to develop a strong internal control capability while you are young?

Discussion Opportunity: For people to live together in an orderly and peaceful way, there must be some form of control to keep their passions in check and to assure fairness in dealings between one another. Possessit and Perverter try to persuade people that what they want is more important than what other people want, and that whatever they do to get what they want is ok. When they succeed, Passionata enters the fray, inflaming feelings to the point where Polarizer can make people enemies of each other. Whole nations are even now in the process of self-destruction because the people have not sufficient internal control and the nations have not been able to develop effective external controls. Character Traits: SR self-reliance; RO caring, citizenship; T honesty, dependability

---

CHOOSING TO BE RESPONSIBLE

Section Three

LEARNING OBJECTIVES FOR SECTION THREE

Understand the four elements of Personal Responsibility

    The Ability to Act

    The Right to Act

    The Duty to Act, and

    Accountability for Acting

Take ownership of thoughts and feelings (attitudes)

Take ownership of choices and actions

SECTION OVERVIEW

The Annual Report to the Board of Overseers of Harvard University on January 11, 1943 stated that "The primary concern of American education today is. . . .to cultivate in the largest possible number of our future citizens an appreciation of both the responsibilities and the benefits which come to them because they are Americans and are free."

As Americans, we frequently concern ourselves with the rights of citizenship and are quick to claim its benefits. But just as frequently we fail to concern ourselves with its responsibilities. Yet, the freedoms we so highly prize are entirely dependent on the responsible exercise of the rights we claim. As Benjamin Franklin wrote, "Only a virtuous people are capable of freedom. As nations become corrupt and vicious, they have more need of masters."

Responsibility is about taking ownership of our choices and actions, it consists of the ability to act, the right to act, the duty to act, and accepting accountability.

The Ability to Act

Each of us is an independent agent, capable of causing things to happen, both good and bad. How we choose to use this ability determines the course of our lives and the kind of people we become. This ability is unique to each person and is the direct result of the connection between an individual's brain and his or her body.

The Right to Act

The ability to act does not confer the right to act. There are many things we are able to do that we have no right to do. The Declaration of Independence proclaims that life, liberty, and the pursuit of happiness is a universal right. As such, each of us has the right to preserve and pursue these rights for ourselves and loved ones. But we can only do so in a manner that does not deny these same rights to anyone else.

The Duty to Act

Personal responsibility largely consists of obligations or duties imposed upon us by the very nature of our own existence. The obligation to choose what we believe, to decide how we will act, and to determine what we will become can never be escaped, ignored, or delegated without penalty. No one else can think what we think, feel what we feel, believe what we believe, or do what we do.

In addition, when others are dependent on us and we are in positions of trust, we have the duty to act in a manner that will justify that trust.

Accepting Accountability

Having granted us the ability and right to think and act for ourselves nature, in turn, holds us answerable for our use of this capacity. We are also answerable to others when we violate their rights.

Thus it is, that only by taking personal ownership of our thoughts, feelings, and actions are we ever able to achieve our full potential.

ACTIVITY 41

WASHINGTON'S MAXIMS

ADVANCE PREPARATION: *Photocopy page 93 for each student.*

In handing out the worksheet, explain that as a young boy, George Washington had a notebook in which he wrote 110 maxims or rules of conduct he wished to follow. He titled the list, "Rules of Civility and Decent Behavior." On the worksheet are five of the rules of conduct, or maxims, Washington chose to guide his life. To the right of each maxim is a space for students to fill in what they think the benefits of following that rule of conduct might be. On the lower half of the page is a place for them to write in five rules of conduct they personally wish to follow and the benefits they think would be associated with following each of those rules of conduct.

Hindsight Questions
- What is a maxim or rule of conduct?

Insight Questions
- Why do you think Washington wrote out these rules of conduct for himself?
- What is there about about these rules that make you think Washington took ownership of his choices?

Foresight Questions
- How can establishing rules of conduct for yourself make certain choices easier when you later have to make them?

Discussion Opportunity: One of the things that made George Washington such a great leader is that, while still a child, he established certain rules of conduct for himself, rules that guided him in choosing things he would say and do and things he would neither say nor do. In later life, these rules proved invaluable to him as General and Commander in Chief of the Continental Army and later as the first President of the United States. He accepted these responsibilities as a matter of duty and not as positions for personal advancement. Possessit was unable to infect him with the "I Want Bias" even, when some were trying to make him a King. When Prevaricator tried to spread lies about him, his reputation for honesty protected him. When Perverter attempted to befog his understanding, he was able to keep perspective. Passionata could not turn discouragement into fear or disagreement into hate. Even though he was engaged in war, Polarizer could not make him enemies with persons, only with principles, and then only in self-defense. Early in life, Washington had taken ownership of his thoughts and feelings, and EPT could not take that from him. Character Traits: PR duty, ownership; SR self-understanding, self-reliance, RO citizenship; T honesty.

Rules of Civility and Decent Behavior

Maxim	Benefit
Associate yourself with persons of good character. It is better to be alone than in bad company.	
Accept corrections thankfully.	
Labor to keep alive in your breast that little spark of celestial fire called conscience.	
Speak not injurious words, either in jest or in earnest.	
Reproach none for the infirmities of nature.	

Five Rules I Want to Live By

Rule 1: _____

Benefit: _____

Rule 2: _____

Benefit: _____

Rule 3: _____

Benefit: _____

Rule 4: _____

Benefit: _____

Rule 5: _____

Benefit: _____

ACTIVITY 42

THE CHICKEN AND THE EAGLE

by George L. Rogers

The chicken and the eagle were standing there one day,
Looking each one over and wondering what to say.
The eagle said, "I.., I've seen things to day I've never seen before."
And quietly, the chicken waited, for her friend to tell her more.

The day had started for them much like any other day,
Both eating corn and pecking grain in the usual chicken way.
They lived together in a barnyard midst other flock and herd,
For here the eagle had been brought when just a baby bird.

They had grown up together, as the very best of friends,
And both thought they were chickens, just ordinary hens.
But now it was different, for today the eagle had flown,
And both knew the little barnyard would no longer be her home.

"I saw such wondrous sights!" said the eagle to her friend.
"There were mountains and streams and fields without end.
There were all kinds of creatures as far as I could see,
And the whole earth it seemed was spread out before me."

The chicken marveled at what her friend had seen while sailing in the sky,
But she knew that she would never see them, for she too had tried to fly.
"I shall miss you dreadfully," said the chicken to her friend
"No longer will I be content, in this barnyard to be penned."

"But I'm glad that you're an eagle, that you at least can fly,
And can see the sights I'll never see while soaring through the sky.
Then the chicken bowed her head in sorrow at the thought,
And tried to be glad her eagle friend was all that she was not.

"Yes my friend, but have you ever thought," said the Eagle to the hen,
The importance of the life you live within your barnyard pen?
It's true, I guess, many great sights I'll be able to see,
But 'twill be of no great benefit to anyone but me."

"You may never see such wonders," said the eagle to her friend,
But now I know while standing here, you have a higher end.
For all that you require in water, a little grain, and a place to live,
You'll pay back a hundredfold in everything you give.

"For every morn at crack of dawn, in a quiet, unnoticed way,
You nourish both old and young with every egg you lay.
And though it may seem exciting to fly up high and free,
It's chickens, not eagles, that feed the world you see.

Though now you may envy me, said the eagle with tearful eye,
Just remember that as we live so shall we die.
My life, though more glamorous it may seem to you,
Will serve far less purpose than anything that you may do.

The two friends looked at each other, they knew the time had come,
And in a quiet voice the chicken spoke, with affection to her chum,
"Thanks to you I can go forward now and do my duty to the end,
And know that I'm a better chicken now, because once I had an eagle friend."

Hindsight Questions
- How did the chicken learn it could not fly?
- How did that discovery make the chicken feel?
- What did the Eagle say to the Chicken that made her feel better?

Insight Questions
- Why does it seem more glamorous to be an eagle than a chicken?
- In the nature of things, what kinds of creatures are eagles?
- Why are chickens far more useful birds than eagles?

Foresight Questions
- How does this little story relate to choices you may have to make?
- Where is the glory in doing one's duty?

Discussion Opportunity: There is a place in the world for both chickens and eagles, but Perverter will try to exaggerate the qualities of the eagle and minimize the qualities of the chicken. In the nature of things, the eagle is a predatory, self-serving creature, adding little to the world but the beauty of its flight. The ordinary chicken, laying its daily egg, by this simple act provides immeasurable benefits to the world around it. So it is with people. Society stands on the legs of its ordinary citizens doing their duty and living responsibly on a daily basis. Character Traits: PR duty; SR self-understanding

ACTIVITY 43

THE HANDSOME AND THE UGLY LEG

Adapted from Benjamin Franklin's *The Handsome and Deformed Leg*

There are two sorts of people in the world, and though they may be equal in health, wealth, and other comforts of life, the one is happy and the other miserable. This arises from the different views in which they consider people and things.

I have an old friend who made use of his legs to tell the difference between these two kinds of people. It so happened that one of his legs was remarkably handsome, but his other leg, by some accident of nature was crooked and deformed. If a person took more notice of his ugly leg than of his handsome one, my friend concluded this person was inclined to be of the complaining sort. He resolved this was not the kind of person he wanted to be around. On the other hand, if a person paid more attention to his handsome leg than to the ugly leg, he believed this person was more likely to be of the cheerful and pleasant sort. This was the kind of person whose friendship he welcomed.

In every situation in life people may find things to like or dislike. Foods may be considered more or less tasty. Activities may be thought more or less fun. People may seem more or less friendly. Topics may be more or less interesting, and the weather more or less pleasing. In almost every face and every person, it is possible discover both good and bad qualities. In short, wherever they are, whatever they're doing, and whoever they're with, people may find things to either like or dislike.

In every case, the happy are happy and the miserable are miserable, not because of where they are or what they are doing, but because of where they fix their attention. People who are happy fix their attention on the pleasant parts of things. They find reason to enjoy their food, to appreciate their associates, and to find good in their circumstances, and thus they cheerfully enjoy all.

People who are unhappy, on the other hand, think and speak only of negative things. Though mostly an act of imagination, the tendency to criticize nevertheless brings about real unhappiness. People of this sort dwell on what they suppose to be wrong in everyone and everything. Hence, they are continually discontented. By their remarks they frequently sour their relationships with other people, offending many and generally making themselves disagreeable to be around.

Consider how distasteful it is to be around people who are complaining, whining, or tearing other people down. Consider how unpleasant is to associate with those who constantly bicker, quarrel, and fight. On the other hand, consider how well loved are people who treat others with cheerfulness and friendliness, and who are thoughtful and considerate of others.

So, should you ever feel discontented and generally unhappy, and find life less satisfying than you might like, you may discover signs of a fault-finding disposition operating within yourself. I say, should this happen and you would like to feel more happy with yourself and be more loved by others, I would simply advise you to quit looking at the ugly leg and fix your attention on the one more handsome.

Hindsight Questions
- Why did Franklin think some people are less happy than others?
- What did he think they could do to become more happy?

Insight Questions
- What does, "In every situation in life people may find things to like or dislike." mean?"
- Why does it matter where we fix our attention?

Foresight Questions
- What choice is Franklin recommending we make in this essay?
- How is this an example of taking ownership of our thoughts, feelings and actions?

Discussion Opportunity: How we look at things makes a huge difference in the quality of life we experience. That's why members of EPT try to get us to focus on the ugly side of things. It is only by taking ownership of our thoughts and feelings that we can escape their influence. Character Traits: PR ownership

ACTIVITY 44

ANIMAL ATTITUDES PICTIONARY

Write the following phrases on separate pieces of paper. Invite one student at a time to draw pictures on the board to provide clues to help the other students guess the phrase. To add interest divide into teams.

Eager beaver	Bright eyed and bushy tailed
Stubborn as a mule	Busy as a bee
Sly as a fox	Quiet as a mouse

Hindsight Questions
- What is the meaning of each of these statements?
- What are they intended to describe?

Insight Questions
- How are human behaviors very different from animal behaviors or characteristics?
- To what extent can a person choose to be enthusiastic and hardworking?

Foresight Questions
- Why might a person choose to be enthusiastic and hardworking?
- What does taking ownership of your thoughts and feelings enable you to do?

Discussion Opportunity: Humans have a great deal of choice as to the kind of individuals they want to be. Perverter may try to make your problems seem insurmountable and your opportunities seem very small. Polarizer may try to pit you against other people. Possessit may try to get you to want things that aren't good for you. But you can choose whether to believe them. By using the seven C skills you can take ownership of your thoughts and feelings. Character Traits: PR ownership

BIOGRAPHY

AL AND IRENE

They were born just a few months apart. She in Paris, France in 1897. He in New York City in 1899. She lived to be 58 and he died at the age of 48. Their lives spanned the first half of the twentieth century. In was a time of new discoveries and invention. During their life times the automobile, the airplane, the telephone, and electric lighting all came into common usage. They lived during a period of great progress in science, medicine, commerce, and communication. Both were were destined to achieve world fame and recognition for what they did and how they used their lives.

Irene was a good student in school and diligently applied herself to her studies. Al had little interest in school, and more often than not played hooky. While she was learning her lessons in the classroom, he was learning his in the street. By the time they were eighteen years old, great differences existed in their approach to life. When she was eighteen, Irene was working alone in a Anglo-Belgian field hospital only a few kilometers from the front lines during World War I. Her job was to teach the hospital staff how to use X- rays in removing shrapnel and setting broken bones. Her greatest challenge was in overcoming the skepticism and resistance of the military surgeons to the use of this new technology. But Irene was up to the task, and many lives were saved because of her efforts.

When Al was eighteen, he committed his first murder. An acquaintance of his had just won $1,500 in a local crap game. Later, downstairs in a hallway, Al poked a gun in in his belly and took the money.

"You oughta be ashamed doing this to me. I know you good!" the fellow said.

Al took this as a threat and pulled the trigger.

"The kid was wrong," he later explained to his gangland boss, Frankie Yale, "He never should have said that, it was the wrong thing to say. It was his own fault he got shot."

By 1925, both Irene Curie and Al Capone were well launched into the careers that would bring them fame and world recognition. This was the year Irene presented her doctoral dissertation on alpha particles emitted by radioactive polonium as it disintegrates. Al, on the other hand was up to his ears in a gangland war.

By this time, Al had moved to Chicago where he had risen to become the head of a crime syndicate. With his former boss, John Torrio, Capone had brought together rival gangs and had divided Chicago into separate territories. Each gang had its own specific area in which to sell liquor, and to run gambling and other criminal operations. Torrio and Capone provided the liquor and protection from the police. They made sure officials in city government and the police force were paid handsomely to look the other way when any of their "boys" were involved in a crime.

The problem Capone had was that different gangs kept trying to muscle in on each others territory. It was Al's job to keep them in line. He was aided in this responsibility by a new invention, the Thompson sub-machine gun.

The number of dead in the gangland war ran high, but when it was over, Al Capone emerged clearly on top. By 1927, Al was a celebrity and his name was known, if not admired, throughout the world. During these years, Irene was working quietly in her laboratory virtually unknown to anyone except as Madam Curie's daughter.

1934 was a big year for both Al and Irene. For Irene, it was the year she and her husband Fred discovered artificial radioactivity which led to their receiving the Nobel Prize in Chemistry the following year. For Al, it was the year he entered Alcatraz. In 1932, Al had been imprisoned for tax evasion, but while at the US Penitentiary in Atlanta, he was accused of receiving special privileges and of continuing to run his organization from behind bars. On August 22, 1934, Al was one of fifty-three prisoners transferred from the penitentiary at Atlanta to become the first inmates of that island prison. In Alcatraz, Al was literally cut off from the outside world. No newspapers, no radio, no visitors other than immediate family, and that only by special arrangement and under careful supervision.

When he finally left prison in November of 1939, after serving only seven of an eleven year sentence, Al Capone was but a shadow of his former self. Venereal disease had robbed him of most of his mental capacity, and he lived out the rest of his life in a state of mental incompetence.

While Capone was wasting away, Irene and her husband, as others in France, were caught up in World War II. Fred, her husband became active in the French resistance movement while Irene held together their family and protected their laboratory. After the war, Irene continued to be active in scientific research, in politics, and in internationally espousing peace and women's rights issues until the time of her death.

Hindsight Questions
- How did Irene Curie's life differ from that of Al Capone?

Insight Questions
- How was Al Capone held accountable for his choices?
- What makes you think he did not take ownership for his choices.

Foresight Questions
- At the end of their lives, which do you think could look back with the greatest satisfaction?

> **Discussion Opportunity:** Al Capone chose to do things he had the ability to do, but no right to do. In addition, he refused to take ownership of his choice. For example, when he killed the man he robbed, he blamed in on the man he killed. Only agents from EPT could get a person to think something like that. In the end, Capone was held accountable for his choices by both the laws of man and the laws of nature. On the other hand, Irene took ownership of her choices. She acted within her right to act, did her duty as well as she could, and in the end, was rewarded for her efforts in a far different way than Al Capone. To help her achieve her goals, she relied heavily on the C skills of criticism, concentration, creativity, and curiosity. Character Traits: PR right, duty, ownership, accountability; SR self-denial, self-reliance; RO caring, citizenship; T honesty

ACTIVITY 46

FAMILIAR SITUATION PANTOMIMES

Invite students to pantomime each of the following situations for the class to guess what the person is doing.

1) A student socializing in class and not paying attention.
2) A shoe maker taking pride in his work.
3) A cheerful person washing a window.
4) A grumpy person who just woke up.

After the activity, ask and discuss:
- Which of these people were taking ownership of their thoughts, feelings and choices?

BIOGRAPHY

THE LAST OF THE HUMAN FREEDOMS

Adapted from Vicktor Frankl's *Man's Search for Meaning*

This was not something for which his training as a psychiatrist had prepared him. He was one of 1500 people, stuffed 80 to a coach, on a train destined for where, he knew not. After several days, the train slowed to a stop. One of the passengers saw a sign. It read "Auschwitz!" Auschwitz—the very name stood for every horror the mind could conceive. Gas chambers, crematoriums, massacres! As the passengers stepped from the train, a Secret Service officer, with a flick of his finger, directed each person to go either to the left or to the right. Most were directed to the left. Viktor Frankl was directed to the right, and thus began his painful descent into a human hell where all rules of civilized society had ceased to exist.

Frankl and others sent to the right were herded to a building in which they were commanded to strip off all clothing and where they were completely shaved of all body hair. Standing there—huddled with a group of frightened, naked men and stripped of all possessions except his glasses and a belt—Frankl became painfully aware that all he had remaining of his former life was his bare, naked existence.

Later that evening, Frankl inquired of some prisoners who had been in Auschwitz for some time where a friend who had been with him on the train might be. Frankl was asked if his friend had been sent to the left side. When Frankl answered yes, one of the prisoners said, "Then you can see him there," pointing to a chimney spewing flames and smoke into the sky just a few hundred yards from where they were standing. Still not understanding, Frankl had to be told in plain terms that his friend and the hundreds of others who had been sent to the left were already dead. It was their ashes spewing from the flames.

In camp, those prisoners who were kept alive were subjected to frequent beatings, filthy condi-

tions, scant food, and hard physical labor. Frankl noted, however, that not all prisoners responded to their circumstances in the same manner. There were Capos, prisoners the SS had selected to be supervisors. Capos often became more vicious in beating other prisoners than were the guards. They were selected only from individuals whose character made them suitable for such procedures. Frankl observed, however, that in addition to the selection process used by the SS, there was also a sort of self-selection process going on. He discovered that there were those who "were prepared to use every means, honest and otherwise, even brutal force, theft, and betrayal of friends, in order to save themselves." But then there were others, "men who walked through the huts comforting others, [and] giving away their last piece of bread." Frankl observed that even in these extreme conditions of inadequate rest, lack of food, and severe stress, "the sort of person the prisoner became was the result of inner decision, and not the result of camp influences alone."

Although only a few of those prisoners Frankl observed achieved the high moral standard of which they were capable, Frankl concluded, "they offer sufficient proof that everything can be taken from a man but one thing: the last of the human freedoms—to choose one's attitude in any given set of circumstances, to choose one's own way."

Frankl survived his experience in the death camps and devoted his professional career to the study of why prisoners, and others, react so differently when exposed to essentially the same circumstances. Frankl's conclusions are best summarized by a quote from the German philosopher, Fredrich Wilhelm Nietzsche: "He who has a why to live can bear with almost any how."

Hindsight Questions
- Frankl observed a sort of self-selection process taking place. What did he observe?
- What was the last of the human freedoms to which Frankl referred?

Insight Questions
- Though robbed of freedom and even the most basic of needs and comforts, what kinds of choices could the prisoners still make?

Foresight Questions
- How can you apply the lesson Frankl learned in your own lives?

Discussion Opportunity: Viktor Frankl was suddenly robbed of everything but his bare existence. Others with him were even robbed of that. Certainly his captors did not have the right to cast he and others into prison camps and to exterminate those who were not useful to them as slaves. But, that was not much comfort to Frankl and those who were imprisoned with him. They had to draw on deeper reserves to cope with their situations. There were those whose highest goal was to survive and who would use any means available to do so. But there were some who had a higher goal. They were more concerned with what kind of lives they lived than how long they lived. Drawing on the C skill of Criticism, Frankl observed this choice was the result of an inner decision not affected by external circumstances. Character Traits: PR right, ownership; RO caring, citizenship

---

ACTIVITY 48

THE TFAC CONNECTION

ADVANCE PREPARATION: *Photocopy the TFAC Activity Sheet on page 102 for students.*

Explain that the T-F-A-C Connection is this: Thoughts and Feelings (Attitudes) generate Actions which, in turn, create Consequences. Have students fill in the blanks and then discuss both their answers and the HIF questions below.

Hindsight Questions
- What did you learn from the TFAC Connection?

Insight Questions
- What is the connection between thoughts and feelings (attitudes), actions, and consequences?
- Of the four, which do you have any choice about?
- Of the four, which two will give you the greatest control over the outcome?

Foresight Questions
- Why is it important to consider consequences before choosing any action?

T-F-A-C Work Sheet

In each of the following situations, fill in the empty squares by writing what you think the person might be either thinking, feeling, or doing, or what you think the possible consequences of their actions might be.

I Think	I Feel	I Act	Possible Consequences
Amy forgot her lunch		Share lunch with Amy	
	Extremely tired, but very determined		Completes mile swim
That man dropped his wallet		Make sure no one is looking, then put wallet in pocket and run away.	
	Angry at my little brother.		Brother is hurt and crying.
		Jump into swimming pool and save small child from drowning.	Personal happiness. Grateful parents of child.
This medicine tastes terrible. I won't take it.		Refuse to take medicine for pneumonia	

ACTIVITY 49

THERE ARE REALLY WOLVES

The Aesop Fable *The Boy Who Cried Wolf* retold by George L. Rogers

The boy was there for a purpose, but, he couldn't tell you what,
And the reason? Well, let's just say, he gave it little thought.
It's true, that all his family owned was entrusted to his care,
But none of this was on his mind, this shepherd boy while sitting there.

The sheep were grazing peacefully in a meadow on the hill,
The day was warm and quiet, and all was calm and still.
The boy was bored and uninvolved, he wanted something else to do,
"I'm going to have some fun," he thought, "before this day is though."

"I know what I'll do he said, I'll trick the villagers in the dell."
So, jumping up he hollered, "Wolf! Wolf!" as loud as he could yell.
Soon came running merchants and farmers and townspeople too,
All waving their sticks and beating on pans, as up the hill they flew.

Huffing and puffing they arrived at the top, just in time to see,
Surrounded by sheep, this shepherd boy, laughing and dancing with glee.
That was the funniest thing I ever saw, he giggled as he spoke,
But as you can see there was no wolf, the wolf was just a joke.

Angry were they with that shepherd boy, that he should treat them so,
Fussing and fuming, those who had come, returned to their village below.
But as the day wore on, the shepherd boy, more mischief did conceive,
And when the frightful cry of "Wolf!" was heard, again they did believe.

Again, running with sticks and beating on pans, up the hill so steep,
The villagers all came to help the boy defend his flock of sheep.
But, oh my oh my, unhappy were they, at his silly ploy,
When they found again they had been taken in, by this shepherd boy.

Yet, one more time the villagers, this foolish boy deceived,
When one more time his cry of "Wolf!", was one more time believed,
And, one more time the villagers, to his aid did run,
To find once more his call for help, was merely made in fun.

But, as so often when thoughtless deeds are done,
And serious acts are taken, all in the name of fun,
The thing it was they really did, so many often find,
Is very, very different than, the thing they had in mind.

So it was with our shepherd boy, lulled by this peaceful scene,
To forget somehow, there are really wolves; hungry, vicious, and mean.
But they were there and sure enough, they found his sheep on the hill,
And carefully surrounding his flock, patiently they closed in for the kill.

Ferocious growling and fearful bleating awoke the boy from sleep,
When all at once, as on a cue, the wolves attacked his sheep.
The fierce nature of this savage attack, filled his heart with fright,
And the shepherd boy began to yell, "Wolf!" "Wolf!" with all his soul and might.

But alas, no one came to help him from the village in the dell,
For, when the shepherd boy cried "Wolf!" as loud as he could yell,
No one believed his cry for help, and so they said, "We're through,
We've played this silly game enough, we've other things to do!"

So there he was, all alone on the hill, unable to help his sheep,
All he could do was stand there and watch and wail and weep.
And so he learned that fateful day, those who are most deceived,
Are those who do not tell the truth and cannot be believed.

Hindsight Questions
- What was the Shepherd boy's duty?

Insight Questions
- What did the shepherd boy minimize? exaggerate?

Foresight Questions
- What can you learn from the story of the boy who cried wolf?

Discussion Opportunity: Obviously the shepherd boy did not possess the C skills. Perverter was able to befog his thinking with Puff Belarge and Puff Belittle. There was no risk from wolves he thought, nor did he seem to care much about the villagers feelings. He never even considered the possibility of losing all his sheep or the effect it would have on his family. The only thing that seemed important to him was having a little fun. That was what he wanted. And in retrospect the fun was little enough for the price he paid. Criticism could have helped him to be more thoughtful of his duty to his family and more considerate of others. Curiosity could have made him wonder if there were wolves near and what might happen if they did attack the sheep. Creativity could have helped him come up with more appropriate ways to have fun. Character Traits: PR duty, ownership, accountability; SR self-reliance; T honesty, dependability

ACTIVITY 50

BIOGRAPHY

I PLEAD GUILTY TO ALL THE CHARGES

The small, skinny man with brown skin, lightly clad in a white loin cloth, sat quietly in the jail thinking. He had been arrested shortly after midnight while sleeping under an old mango tree at his camp in Karadi. Without trial and without sentence, he had simply been put behind bars. The Viceroy apparently did not want to risk another trial in which Gandhi could make another courtroom speech. Gandhi smiled as he considered the success of his strategy. He likened his march to the sea to the Boston Tea Party which had taken place in America over a hundred and fifty years earlier.

As a leader, Gandhi understood the people of India better than any other. He lived with them and shared their poverty. He talked with them in their fields and in their factories. He had found among these impoverished, illiterate masses some of the noblest individuals he had ever known. He knew they loved their families. He knew they had thoughts, feelings and yearnings for a better life. He knew they were willing to work, but needed the means and the opportunity to do so.

The people admired and respected Gandhi in return. He did not live in luxurious surroundings as did so many others who wanted to be their leaders. He lived simply. He ate simple food. He wore simple clothing. There was nothing pretentious about him. Even his strategy was simple—opposition to British rule by non-violent civil disobedience. No government can impose laws against the will of the people if the people resist in mass. But, neither can just laws be established when the people are violent, lawless, and destructive of human life. Even Gandhi's plan to involve the people was simple.

After all, it was a simple gesture, to make a few grains of salt from sea water. Even a child could do it. But, it was for this reason, Gandhi

had led a march of two hundred miles to the sea. The act was simple, but it was an open act of defiance against one of the many laws designed to make the British wealthy. Laws which drained from his people the small profits of their meager existence, keeping them always poor and on the edge of starvation. The salt law was an obvious example. In India, everyone needed salt, but under the salt law, only the government could manufacture salt. Despite the fact that salt was easy to make, the people had to buy all their salt from the government.

Gandhi had advised the Viceroy that he would be making the march. He pointed out the unjustness of the law and even called attention to the fact that the Viceroy enjoyed a salary of $7,000 a month while the average income for an Indian was only 4 cents per day. Gandhi had respectfully invited the Viceroy to meet with him so that it would not be necessary for him to make this march. But, Gandhi had also warned the Viceroy that if he would not work with him to find more just methods for governing India, then he would undertake the march to the sea with as many as would be willing to march with him.

The Viceroy had decided to ignore Gandhi. He felt the march would be meaningless, that no one would care. Sitting in the jail, Gandhi smiled as he thought about how the number of marchers had swelled to several thousand by the time they had reached the sea. In every village they had passed through, hundreds of villagers had left their work to join them. On the beach, amid the cheers of this vast throng, Gandhi had made a pinch of salt. It wasn't the quantity that mattered, only the act. After the march, throughout India, people began making salt. The government crackdown was severe, even brutal. But his fellow Indians had continued to make salt even while submitting to the beatings and to the mass arrests without resisting. Throughout India, jails were filled to overflowing, but the people continued making salt.

As Gandhi sat there, he reflected upon the first time he was sent to jail in eight years previously, in March of 1922. In the courtroom that day, Gandhi had told the judge, "I plead guilty to all the charges." He felt the same today.

In his statement to the court that day, Gandhi had explained why he was no longer a loyal English subject, but an open and outspoken opponent of British rule in India. He recounted to the judge how, as an Indian in South Africa, he discovered that he did not have the same rights as other Englishmen. Although he had gone to the same law schools, he could not practice law on the same basis as other Englishmen. He couldn't even ride the in the same rail cars as other Englishmen. He had discovered that because he was an Indian, he had no right as a man. He had explained to the judge that day how his opposition to the system of government imposed on India continued to grow as he became increasingly aware of the broad based system of injustice it practiced on the people.

"I came reluctantly to the conclusion," he had said, "that the British connection had made India more helpless than she was before, politically and economically. India has become so poor that she has little power of even resisting famines. . . . Little do town dwellers know how the semi-starved masses of India are slowly sinking to lifelessness. Little do they know that their miserable condition is the result of having the profits of their labors sucked away into British pockets. Little do they realize that the government established by law in British India is carried on for the exploitation of the masses. No fancy words, no juggling figures can explain away the evidence that the skeletons in many villages present to the naked eye."

That was eight long years ago. He had been in prison many times since then, but now Gandhi felt his people were ready to stand up for their rights, and to do it without resorting to the same violent and destructive tactics the British used. Gandhi, smiled. He was confident he would see India free within his life time. It would not be easy. Nor would it come without suffering. But it would come. Gandhi knew what the British still did not understand, that any system of government that impoverishes the masses to enrich a favored few, cannot long endure.

Hindsight Questions
- Why did Gandhi march two hundred miles to the sea to make a pinch of salt?
- Why was Gandhi opposed to British rule?

Insight Questions
- Why was the law that prevented ordinary Indians from making salt unjust?
- Why did Gandhi feel British rule was weakening his people?

Foresight Questions
- Why did Gandhi feel civil disobedience needed to be non-violent?
- What happens when people use violence to get what they want?

Discussion Opportunity: Possessit convinced the British they were the rightful rulers of India and that they were entitled to the wealth and advantages such a position provided. Polarizer and Passionata were working hard to stir up enmity and violence between the British and their Indian subjects. But Gandhi knew the power of self-control. Criticism had enabled him to observe the destructive tendencies of violence. He was also keenly aware that British rule was slowly destroying his people. Creativity helped him devise ways of helping his people restore their dignity and claim their rights without themselves resorting to violence. For, he knew that in the end, this would be the only way his country would be fit for self-government. Character Traits: PR right, ownership; SR self-understanding, self-reliance; RO caring, fairness, citizenship; T honesty, dependability

CHOOSING TO RESPECT MYSELF

Section Four

LEARNING OBJECTIVES FOR SECTION FOUR

Recognize the Importance of Having Self-Respect

Identify Four Areas of Conduct that Will Create Self-Respect

Self-Understanding

Self-Denial

Self-Reliance

Selflessness

Desire to Possess Self-Respect

SECTION OVERVIEW

Benjamin Franklin wrote, "There is no happiness but in a virtuous and self-approving conduct." In the same place, he also wrote, "What is without us has not the least connection with happiness only so far as the preservation of our lives and health depends upon it." Unfortunately, all too many look for self-respect in the approval of others, often by doing things they cannot approve of themselves. But in the nature of things; self-respect can only be found within and, only then, as the result of a virtuous and self-approving conduct.

Four general areas of conduct may be relied on to help produce self-respect. They are self-understanding, self-denial, self-reliance, and selflessness.

Self-Understanding

To fully achieve your potential, it is important to understand two things: your strengths and your weaknesses. Strengths are what you must build on, weaknesses are what you must build around. Nature has endowed each of us with unique talents and gifts, which when used for virtuous purposes can produce satisfactions not achievable in any other way. At the same time, each of us has weaknesses. If we understand our weaknesses, we can generally find ways to work around or overcome them. For example, Thomas Edison was not good at math. For an inventor, this could be a serious shortcoming. His solution? Hire people who were good at math to work for him. Frederick Douglass didn't know how to read or write. His solution? Enlist other children to teach him.

Self-Denial

We all want things that would not be good for us if we got them. It is nearly impossible to do something you know is not good for you and still have self-respect. Indulging in harmful activities and substances creates feelings of weakness and guilt while denying oneself these things creates feelings of strength and freedom.

Self-Reliance

An important source of self-respect is the ability to rely on one's self. To do this requires the exercise of initiative and industriousness. It also requires a measure of independence, persistence, and patience in performing tasks and pursuing goals.

Selflessness

It has been said the best way to find oneself is in the service of others. This is because there is more of you to find. Few things can build self-respect better than doing good to others.

ACTIVITY 51

SELF-RESPECT, A PREREQUISITE FOR RESPECTING OTHERS
Chalk Talk

List three columns on the board. In the first write the set of behaviors listed below and ask why people do these things. Write their answers under the "Common Reasons" column. Point out that most of these reasons are related to a lack of self-respect. People who feel good about themselves seldom behave in this manner. Then discuss why self-respect is a prerequisite for being able to respect others and fill in third column, "How Self-Respect Helps.".

Behavior	Common Reasons	How Self-Respect Helps
Teasing, Ridiculing, Bullying, Gossiping	An attempt to make one's self seem bigger by making other people seem smaller Feelings of inadequacy, Fear of differences, Jealousy	Self-Understanding removes need to compare self with others, provides better understanding of others, helps increase appreciation of other's needs and feelings
Not sharing, Cheating, Stealing	The "I Want Bias", Selfishness, Feelings of being cheated, Blaming problems on others	Self-Denial, able to do without, unwilling to hurt others; Self-Reliance, able to obtain with honest work
Hurting, Vandalizing, Destroying	Frustrated desires, Feelings of revenge, Not feeling accepted or loved, To demonstrate potency and power	Self-Understanding, recognize sources of frustration and feelings; Self-Denial, able keep feelings under control; Self-Reliant, not dependent on others for recognition

ACTIVITY 52

What Am I? - Habits Activity Sheet

ADVANCE PREPARATION: *Photocopy the activity sheet on page 107 for each student. Have students solve the riddle and complete the rest of the sheet.*

Discussion Opportunity: Self-Respect must be present before the ability to respect others truly exists. Two things that can greatly increase self-respect are a good conscience and good habits. A guilty conscience and bad habits virtually assure a person will not have a high level of self-respect. Character Traits: SR self-understanding, self-denial, self-reliance

WHAT AM I?

Solve the following riddle. Use the solution to fill in the blanks in part two and list five of each. Then fill in the blanks in part three and follow the instructions.

Part 1

I can be weak or strong
But when I'm strong I'm hard to change
I become stronger
Each time something is done in the same way

I can be good or bad
If I'm good I will really help you
But, if I am bad I will surely hurt you
If you don't care whether I'm good or bad
Just follow the course of least resistance
But if you want me to be good
You will have to work to form me as you wish

WHAT AM I? _____

Part 2

NAME FIVE BAD _____

NAME FIVE GOOD _____

Part 3

If _____ are strengthened by frequent repetition and weakened by less frequent repetition, on the back page devise a method for acquiring good _____ and eliminating bad _____.

BIOGRAPHY

FIRST LADY OF THE WORLD

A biographical sketch of Eleanor Roosevelt

Many called her "The First Lady of the World." Certainly she was one of the best known and most loved women in the world. In nominating her for the Nobel Peace Prize, Jean Monnet said of Eleanor Roosevelt, "Her great contribution was her persistence in carrying into practice her deep belief in liberty and equality. She would not accept that anyone should suffer—because they were women, or children, or foreign, or poor, or stateless refugees."

President Harry S. Truman had appointed her to be the U.S. Delegate to the UN Commission on Human Rights. For five years she served as chair of that committee during which time the commission drafted, and the United Nations approved, The Universal Declaration of Human Rights which is still used as the standard of conduct expected of civilized nations. In this and other capacities, both official and unofficial, Eleanor Roosevelt traveled throughout the world and her own country advocating the needs of the downtrodden and oppressed. When Eleanor spoke, it was with the quiet confidence born of conviction and with a clear understanding of what she believed and why.

But Eleanor had not always been confident, either in her opinions or in her manner. In fact it was not until her husband, Franklin, was President of the United States that in many respects her life really began. It was not enough for Eleanor to live in elegance and splendor while so many in the world were suffering with hunger and want. And personal fame meant little to a woman who recognized that large numbers of people were slipping into nameless and silent graves for want of even the most basic of human comforts. After her husband became President, Eleanor felt that she not only had the opportunity, but a particular responsibility to speak out and

to do what she could to correct social injustices she saw about her. From then on, Eleanor was as likely to be seen dishing up food in a soup kitchen for the poor as she was to be seen hosting a dinner for diplomats, to be seen inspecting a mine for safety as she was to be seen at a political rally. Interestingly, it was not from her association with those in high position that Eleanor's self-confidence grew, but rather from her service to those in need. When she had a purpose larger than herself to which she devoted her energies, Eleanor began to blossom and grow.

Eleanor had never been overly impressed with the trappings of wealth and position. Born into a wealthy and prominent family, Eleanor learned early in life that there is little about either wealth or social position that guaranteed a happy childhood. Her parents, though wonderfully popular among the socially elite, were poorly equipped for the responsibilities of parenthood. Her mother, a beautiful woman possessed with grace and charm, could never seem to appreciate this awkward, shy, little girl. "Granny" was the nickname she gave Eleanor. It always made Eleanor feel ashamed and inadequate. Eleanor's father, on the other hand, made her feel special. She loved the way he treated her. Unfortunately, he was seldom around. Troubled with alcoholism, he was sent away to avoid disgrace to the family. All this happened while Eleanor was very young, and mostly she grew up lonely, being raised by governesses and nurses until her mother died when she was eight years old.

For the next several years, Eleanor lived with her grandmother in a gloomy old mansion which had not one room in which a child could play. During those years, Eleanor had few friends and little opportunity to even play with her cousins. Mostly she felt alone, ugly, and very awkward. It was not until she left her grandmother's to go to a boarding school in England that Eleanor began to blossom, finding friends and doing things that she could enjoy. It was here that she grew into the attractive young lady that young Franklin D. Roosevelt choose to marry.

Franklin was handsome, popular, and very outgoing. He was happiest when with friends. But Eleanor continued to be shy and retiring, preferring to be alone. Social events always made her feel uncomfortable and inadequate. Not long after they were married, Eleanor was thrust into the limelight as the wife of one of the most prominent politicians of their day. It was not a role in which she felt much comfort or satisfaction. While she dutifully tried to fill her responsibilities, whether campaigning for Franklin or hosting parties, Eleanor always felt out of her element.

After Franklin became president, and she was first lady, Eleanor arrived at an important conclusion. "No one can make you feel bad about yourself without your consent." she decided. Eleanor decided the time had come for her to be her own person. She realized that she could do the things she thought were important and still support her husband. As Eleanor took interest in the health problems of miners, in helping the unemployed find better work, in visiting the troops in Europe during WWII, in encouraging women to be involved in the political process, and many other activities, she found that her work proved to be a great assistance to her husband. She was able to call to his attention many circumstances which he would otherwise have not been aware of, and in doing so helped him focus upon many issues that helped him become such a popular president.

After Franklin died, Eleanor continued the work she had started. By this time she had become a fearless fighter for those things in which she believed, and most especially for the underdog. Now, Eleanor traveled as easily in high circles as she did among the poor. In both cases her objective was the same, to lift up the downtrodden, and to provide opportunity for those who were oppressed. In her own country, and throughout the world, Eleanor's presence was felt. Surely there was reason to think that this first lady belonged to the world as much as to her nation.

Hindsight Questions
- Why did Eleanor feel uncomfortable around people?
- What conclusion did she arrive at?
- Where did Eleanor choose to use her considerable talents?

Insight Questions
- What happens to you when you focus on or think about things you feel you are not or can't do?
- How did getting involved in serving others help Eleanor feel better about herself?
- Why is it important to have something larger than yourself alone to work for?

Foresight Questions
- How do people eventually discover their potential to do things?
- What happens if people never reach beyond their comfort zones to do things?

Discussion Opportunity: Perverter, with his Puff Belittle befogger tried to make Eleanor feel small and insignificant, while at the same time using Puff Belarger to make her think others were better than she. He nearly succeeded. Had not Criticism helped her realize that "No one can make you feel bad about yourself without your consent," she may never have realized her potential in life. From there Curiosity helped her recognize areas of service she could perform, Creativity helped her figure out what she could do, Correction helped her make the change, and Communication helped her go to work. Of course, Concentration and Control helped as well. Character Traits: PR ownership; SR self-understanding, self-reliance; RO caring, fairness, citizenship

BIOGRAPHY

THE REAL HARDSHIP OF THIS PLACE

A Biographical Sketch of Florence Nightingale written in first person Have your students guess who this person is.

I was born two years before and died fifteen years after Louis Pasteur. We lived through the same time period, and our work, in many ways was closely related. I was born into a family of inherited wealth and my parents lived a life of luxury and leisure. They did not take it well when I told them I wanted to become a nurse. In the mid 1800's nurses had little medical responsibility and were mostly glorified cleaning ladies. Yet, I felt that somehow, in someway, I could do something more useful with my life than to fritter it away in idleness and elegant parties, doing nothing of importance to anyone.

It was very difficult for me to break away from the discouragement of my family. Nevertheless, I began my work in 1844 by reading government reports on sanitary conditions in hospitals and among the laboring classes in England. Not wanting to upset my parents, I worked in secret. Arising before dawn, wrapped in a shawl, and writing by candlelight, day by day I filled notebook after notebook with the facts and information that enabled me to become the first expert on sanitary conditions in hospitals in Europe. Unfortunately, sanitary conditions at this time were not very good. Most hospitals were filthy places in which more people died than became well. But this all took a very long time. It was another nine years before I was actually working in a hospital, and several years more before my work on sanitary conditions became recognized.

Perhaps the most dramatic turn of events came when war broke out between Russia and Great Britain. This was the Crimerian war. Britain was poorly prepared and the British soldiers suffered terribly, especially the sick and wounded. Amputations were performed without anesthetics by surgeons working in the moonlight because they had no lanterns. In the field the wounded lay on the ground or on straw mixed with manure. Those who made it to the barracks hospital found there were no beds. They had no food because there was no kitchen. They could drink no water because there were no cups or buckets to carry it in. All they could do was lie there in long lines, half naked, in blood stained clothing, on a filthy bare floor.

It was to this scene that I was invited to take a party of nurses. We were to assist the army doctors who were there. Nothing ever quite so amazed me as to discover that the doctors resented our coming, and in particular Dr. Hall, the surgeon in charge. Nevertheless, the sheer numbers of patients forced them to accept our help, and help we did. We cleaned the floors, we organized the meals, and most of all we nursed the sick and dying. I made it a rule to never let a man die alone and was the bedside companion of over 2000 men as they died that terrible winter.

Every night and every day, I personally made rounds, cheering, encouraging, and helping the wounded soldiers however I could. Often it was no more than a kind word or a gentle touch, but it all seemed to be appreciated. When I wasn't in the operating room or on the floor, I was writing letters to families of the men. For those who died, I described their last hours and sent home their dying messages. For those still alive, I sent home notes of encouragement and passed messages to mothers, wives, and sweethearts. Doing all this plus my other responsibilities required every capacity I had and eventually broke my health.

But I can truthfully say, the only truly discouraging aspect of my work was the opposition we received from the military medical establishment. It seemed they felt that any form of improvement not initiated by them, made them look bad. In this state of mind I once wrote, ". . . .the real hardship of this place, dear Mr. Herbert, is that we have to do with men who are neither gentlemen nor men of education nor even men of business, nor men of feeling, whose only object is to keep themselves out of blame."

But despite all, progress was made, lives were saved, and eventually major changes in the British medical system resulted from many of the recommendations I made. Who am I?

Hindsight Questions
- What was required of Florence to become a nurse?
- How did the doctor's respond to having the nurses come to help them?
- What did Florence do to overcome this challenge?

Insight Questions
- Why might Florence not have wanted to pursue the same life style as her parents?
- Why do you think the doctors were not receptive to help from the nurses?
- How do you think the families of the soldiers felt about Florence?

Foresight Questions
- What would have happened to Florence if she had not become a nurse?
- What satisfactions do you think Florence may have received from her work?

Discussion Opportunity: To become a nurse in Florence's day was a high risk venture. They were exposed to disease in every form, worked long, thankless hours, and were paid little for their effort. But Florence, like so many others could see a need to find better ways to relieve the suffering of the sick and wanted to help. Florence had to pay a high price for the opportunity to become a nurse. Perverter had a great influence on her parents and even the doctors she was assigned to work with. With a Puff Belittle befogger he was able to minimize the importance of nursing in their minds. Puff Prejudge, and Florence's parents knew she would bring disgrace to the family by lowering herself to this work. With a similar puff the doctor's knew these women would merely get in their way. But the Seven C's overcame all. Curiosity motivated Florence to study information that made her an expert on sanitation in hospitals and learn the skills of nursing as they existed at the time. Concentration and Criticism helped her master the information and Communication enabled her to share it with others. Creativity helped her know what to do to make a difference and Control gave her the ability to overcome the hardships associated with her undertaking. She took ownership of her choices, was willing to deny herself a life of luxury and exhibited all of the qualities of self-reliance. She cared what happened to others and wanted to make a difference. Character Traits: PR ownership; SR self-understanding, self-denial, self-reliance; RO caring, citizenship

---

BIOGRAPHY

ACTIVITY 55

KORCZAK'S ORPHANS

The year was 1942. The day was August 6. Dr. Korczak and the teachers were cleaning up after the breakfast meal. The meal wasn't much, just some potato peels and crusts of old bread, but even in these dark circumstances, Dr. Korczak insisted that the routine not be broken. "It is important for children to have order," he would remind his teachers, many of whom had grown up in the orphanage themselves.

Now, the orphanage was confined within the walls of the Warsaw ghetto. The ghetto was a small section of Warsaw into which some 400,000 Jews were herded and held prisoner by the Nazi's who had invaded Poland at the beginning of World War II. Food allotted to the ghetto was not sufficient to sustain even 200,000 people, so hunger and starvation were constant companions with those who lived there. Almost all of Dr. Korczak's energies these days were devoted to trying to find food for the 192 orphans under his care. It was continually becoming a more and more difficult task.

Suddenly, an SS officer stepped in the house, blew two blasts on a whistle and shouted, "Alle Juden raus!" which meant, "All Jews out!" Dr. Korczak moved quickly to quiet the children's fears, then went into the courtyard to ask for time for the children to pack their belongings. He knew that they were being "relocated" as the German's called it. He even had some inkling that being "relocated" most likely meant they would be taken to some kind of prison camp. Unknown to Korczak and others living in the ghetto, the "relocations" were being conducted by order of Heinrich Himmler and were part of the Nazi program to exterminate all Jews from Europe. The prison camps were actually death camps designed to exterminate large numbers of people. But even within the ghetto, they had seen enough of random killings by Nazi guards to realize that human life, at least that of Jews, had little value to them. His children were given fifteen minutes to get ready and be in the courtyard.

Dr. Korczak had been director of the orphanage since it was first opened in 1912. Trained as a physician, Dr. Korczak was a medical doctor in Children's Hospital when he was approached to head up the orphanage. He leaped at the chance. His first love was children, and even while practicing medicine had become nationally famous as a writer of children's books. When not writing or practicing medicine, Dr. Korczak was found in the poorer sections of Warsaw talking with impoverished children, telling them stories and listening to their sad tales of hunger and abuse. They knew he would always have something for them, even if it was only a piece of candy, a word of encouragement, or a kiss on the forehead. So when he received the offer to head the orphanage, Korczak responded immediately.

Now, after thirty years, his life was his orphan children. Just a few days before, because of his prominence as a writer and Polish citizen, Dr. Korczak had been given an opportunity to leave the ghetto for a safer place to live. He had refused. "My place is with the children." he had replied. "They need me now and I won't leave them."

As the children gathered in the courtyard, Korczak formed them into lines. Then holding a small child in his arms, and another by the hand, he began leading them to the train that would take them to the gas chambers of Treblinka.

When the little procession left the Ghetto and marched out of the of the gate, they were met by more SS guards who were waiting with whips, guns, and dogs. Outside the walls, nearly four thousand other children joined Dr. Korczak's orphans on the dirt field by the railway siding. All were to be stuffed into cattle cars for the long trip to Treblinka.

When the time came to board the cattle cars, Dr. Korczak with his head erect and one child in each hand, led his orphans and their teachers in orderly rows of four. They marched with quiet dignity, a silent procession following the man who loved them as much as they loved him.

Hindsight Questions
- To what did Dr. Korczak devote his life?
- What were the conditions in the orphanage at the time of the evacuation order?
- When offered safety because of his prominence as a Polish citizen, what did Korczak say?

Insight Questions
- Why would Korczak decline personal safety to be with the children?
- Which agents of EPT had taken control of Nazi thinking?

Foresight Questions
- What are some things that might be considered more important than life itself?
- What did you learn from the story of "Korczak's Orphans?"

Discussion Opportunity: Dr. Korczak was a caring man who literally gave his life for the orphan children he loved. While he was alive, he gave his life in service. In the end, he gave his life so he could be with "his children" at the end of theirs. He lived at an extraordinary time. Passionata had so gripped the Nazi regime that they were willing to kill large masses of innocent people. She was able to do so because Prevaricator had led them to believe the lies of their leaders and Perverter had so clouded their understanding, they were incapable of distinguishing right from wrong. Puff Belarge gave them grossly exaggerated thoughts of glory and power. Puff Belittle and they cared nothing for other human beings. Puff Benamed and Jews became their enemies. Puff Prejudge and all Jews were unworthy to live. Polarizer was next, the enemy must be exterminated.—"They are a danger to our society." But, Korczak knew right from wrong. He had no illusions of grandeur or even personal safety. To him the important thing was to be with and protect the orphan children under his care so long as he had the breath and capacity to do so. Never would he be faced with the spectre of a guilty conscience, either from cowardice or cruelty, but rather his reward was the satisfaction of having loved and been loved by the many children he had cared for over the span of more than three decades. Character Traits: SR self-denial, self-reliance, RO caring, citizenship

BIOGRAPHY

ACTIVITY 56

GEORGE WASHINGTON CARVER GOES TO SCHOOL

Moses Carver was awakened by the sound of thundering hooves. He knew the raiders were coming back and realized immediately they were after his black slave Mary. Quickly he ran to her shack, yelling for her to run and hide, but he was too late. As Mary ran out, carrying her infant son in her arms, she and the baby were picked up and carried off by the horsemen. Jim, Mary's other son, escaped detection.

Sick with worry, Moses and his wife Susan, quickly posted a reward for the return of Mary and the child. Susan and Mary were close friends and their relationship was more like that of sisters than one of slave and mistress. A John Bently volunteered to go in search of the mother and child, and set out the very next day.

A few days later, Moses and Mary looked up from their work to see a lone rider coming toward them. Their hearts sank as they recognized the rider as John Bently. "They got off with your slave girl," Bently explained, as he reached behind him and lifted a small bundle which he handed them, "but, I was able to find the baby with some women. The kidnappers had felt the sickly infant was not worth keeping and had abandoned him." Moses and Susan were overjoyed to get the child back and began raising the two boys as if they were their own children.

The Carver family was poor, and George was quite sickly, but the family was happy. George, though not as physically strong as his brother, had an active mind and took a keen interest in plants. He was particularly good at making sick plants well. By the time he was ten years old, he was fondly known by his neighbors as the "Plant Doctor."

George later wrote: "When just a mere tot my very soul thirsted for an education. I literally lived in the woods. I wanted to know every strange stone, flower, insect, bird, or beast. No one could tell me. My only book was an old Webster's Elementary spelling Book. I would seek the answer here without satisfaction. I almost knew the book by heart." But, until he was twelve years of age, George was unable to attend school. The school in his community would not accept blacks. The nearest school that would accept black students was in Neosho, Missouri, over eight miles away.

At twelve, George decided that if he was to ever to get an education, his only choice was to leave home and go to Neosho. "Aunt Susan" cut down a suit of clothes belonging to Moses. With only the clothes he was wearing and a sack of corn dodgers in his hand, this twelve year old boy waved goodbye to the only parents he had ever known and started walking to Neosho.

George spent his first night in Neosho sleeping in a barn near the school. The next day, young George was taken in by Mariah Watkins and her husband Andrew. For four years he helped "Aunt Mariah" with her laundry business and attended school. George was so intent on learning, he would scrub laundry with a book propped in front of him. Eventually, George felt he had learned all he could in the Neosho school. To continue his education, he had to move on.

For the next eleven years George went from one community to another, attending school where he could. Schools that accepted people of color often were not sufficiently advanced to allow him to progress. Schools that were more advanced often would not accept people of color. He attended wherever he was accepted and felt he could learn. To live, George sometimes set up his own laundry business, other times he worked as a farm hand, cook, or whatever he could find.

In 1890, nearly destitute, George almost gave

up. But, a woman recognizing his talent encouraged him to go on. George sold what little he had, and with the proceeds gained admittance to Simpson College in Iowa. With no where else to live and little remaining money, young Carver obtained permission to live in an abandoned shack near the school grounds. He spent his last ten cents on beef suet (hard fat) and cornmeal. His living circumstances were dismal, but George was excited to be back in school.

George would not accept handouts, however teachers and friends helped him get into better living quarters and find opportunities for work. Later, George completed his education in agricultural science at Iowa Agricultural College as a distinguished graduate. From there he became head of the agricultural department of Tuskegee Institute in Alabama.

When George arrived in Tuskegee, he discovered that he had 13 students but no laboratory. He gathered his students and told them that to study agriculture they needed a laboratory. Then, he led them around the neighborhood knocking on doors and to the local junk yard. They came back with bottles, jars, an oil lamp, and other usable items. The bottles were cut down into beakers, the oil lamp became a bunsen burner, an old tea cup and the end of a drapery rod became mortar and pestle for grinding and mixing substances. The Tuskegee agricultural department was in operation.

Over the next 50 years, George Washington Carver taught thousands of students and assisted still other thousands of farmers in improving their agricultural practices. He developed over 300 uses for the peanut in order to help farmers find markets for their crops. Over the years, George financially helped many students who needed assistance. His work brought him into contact and friendship with Franklin D. Roosevelt, Henry Ford, and Thomas Edison. The little black boy, discarded by a band of kidnappers as worthless so long ago, had became one of the most influential and beloved men of his time.

Hindsight Questions
- How old was George when he left home to go to school?
- Why did he have to leave home to go to school?

Insight Questions
- How did George demonstrate the quality of self-reliance in his life?
- What were some obstacles George had to overcome in getting an education?
- Which of the C skills did George use in getting an education and pursuing a career in agriculture?
- What motivated George to work so hard to get an education?

Foresight
- Who benefitted from George's determination to get an education?
- How?

Discussion Opportunity: EPT agents had persuaded many people that black children should not go to the same schools as white children. They tried to persuade George that he should settle for an inferior education. But his desire to learn was far greater than their influence. At a very young age, he took Control of his life. His unbounding Curiosity made him hungry for knowledge. Creativity worked with Control to help him find appropriate education opportunities. Criticism, Concentration, and Communication helped him be a good student. With these skills, George took ownership of his choices and demonstrated all those qualities of initiative, industriousness, persistence, patience, and resourcefulness necessary to success. These qualities were of great value to him as a teacher when he had to find Creative ways to establish a laboratory for his students. Character Traits: PR ownership; SR self-understanding, self-denial, self-reliance; RO caring, citizenship

---

BIOGRAPHY

ACTIVITY 57

THE FRIEND DOWN INSIDE OF ME

Biographical Sketches of Abraham Lincoln

57-1   Eighty-Eight to One

It was September 1863. Missouri was a powder keg ready to blow at any time. It was one of three slave states to remain in the Union, but it was deeply divided and extremists on both sides of the slavery question were pushing their cause.

On one hand, thousands of soldiers returning from defeated Confederate armies were pouring into the state and forming themselves into bands of guerrillas. They raided villages and towns, stole money and horses, burned houses and bridges, and hung Union men.

Governor Gamble had pronounced Lincoln's call for troops as unconstitutional and many complained to Lincoln that his "pro- slavery" government was paralyzing the Federal Government's prosecution of the war.

On the other hand, in July of that year a conservative convention passed an emancipation ordinance to eliminate slavery, an ordinance sure to fire the passions of both opponents and friends. Their activity was such that Governor Gamble complained to Lincoln that the radicals were openly and loudly threatening to overthrow his government.

In between, the one man holding the opposing sides together was General Schofield, a 32-year old physics professor turned warrior. Schofield was firm in in dealing with both sides even handedly. He considered it his job to prevent civil-war from breaking out within the state. The antislavery forces were furious with him for not taking their side.

On September 1, an Emancipation convention was held by antislavery factions in Jefferson City. The convention authorized a delegation of seventy men, one from each county of the state, to travel to Washington to present their demands to President Lincoln. The first and foremost of these demands was for General Schofield to be relieved of his command and replaced with General Butler, whom they believed to be more sympathetic to their cause.

At train stops on the way the committee was met by brass bands and antislavery delegations. Upon arriving in Washington, they were joined by a Committee of Eighteen from Kansas who had been sent with the same mission. The delegation spent the next two days in preparing their address to the President.

At 9 AM on September 30, the 88 delegates presented themselves at the White House. The great doors were opened and after they entered, the doors were closed and locked. At their request, there were to be no reporters or guests. The meeting was to be between them and the President only.

Prior to the meeting, Lincoln had confided to John Hay, his assistant that if they could show him that Schofield had done anything wrong he would have to remove Schofield. But he seriously doubted that was the case. He rather believed they were against Schofield because he would not take their side. He said, "I think I understand the matter perfectly and I cannot do anything contrary to my convictions, to please these men, earnest and powerful as they may be."

Now, he was face to face with them. One against 88. Lincoln later described them to Hay as follows, "They are nearer to me than the other side, in thought and sentiment, though bitterly hostile [to me] personally. They are utterly lawless—the onhandiest devils in the world to deal with—but, after all, their faces are set Zionwards."

The delegation presented their demands in as pressing terms as they could. Enos Clark, one of the delegates, recorded Lincoln's response.

"You gentlemen," Lincoln said among other things, "must bear in mind that in performing the duties of the office I hold I must represent no one section, but I must act for all sections of the Union in trying to maintain the supremacy of the Government. . . .I so desire to conduct the affairs of this administration that if, at the end, when I come to lay down the reins of power, I have lost every other friend on earth, I shall at least have one friend left, and that friend shall be down inside of me."

Hindsight Questions
- What was the delegation trying to get Lincoln to do?

Insight Questions
- Who was the friend down inside of Lincoln?
- Why were people unable to persuade Lincoln to go contrary to his conscience?

Foresight Questions
- Why was Lincoln to determined to keep this friend?
- What happens to people when they act contrary to their conscience?

Discussion Opportunity: Passionata was ruling the choices of many Missourians, and indeed people throughout both the North and South. Perverter was working his confusion by clouding people's view of the issues. By getting people to take extreme positions on both sides he set the stage for Polarizer to step in and make them enemies. Possessit convinced many that if they didn't get their way, the only solution was violence. EPT agents had a great strangle hold on the state and nation. But, Lincoln was a leader who possessed strong C skills. A superb Communicator, Lincoln had also developed the skills of Criticism and Control to a very high level. His clarity in sorting out difficult issues and ability to work with people in a balanced, fair manner made him a highly effective leader. But, nothing gave him greater strength than his unwillingness to offend his own conscience. Character Traits: PR duty, right, ownership; SR self-understanding, self-denial, self-reliance, RO caring, fairness, citizenship; T honesty

---

57-2   I Never Use Any Man's Money But My Own

At the age of 24, Abraham Lincoln was postmaster of the little frontier village of New Salem, Illinois. For this he received an annual salary of $55.70. The post office was closed in 1836, but it was several years before the Postal service sent an agent from Washington to settle the accounts with the ex-postmaster. By this time he was a struggling lawyer who was not doing well financially.

After examining the books, the agent informed Lincoln a total of $17 was due to the government from receipts of the post office. Lincoln stood up and walked to an old trunk, took out a yellow cotton cloth tied with string and set it on the table. He untied the cloth and spread the money on the table—exactly $17 dollars. When the agent expressed surprise, Lincoln answered, "I never use any man's money but my own."

57-3 The Promise

One day, Lincoln was riding in a stage coach with a colonel from Kentucky. After riding for a while, the colonel removed a bottle of whiskey from his coat and offered Lincoln a drink. Lincoln declined replying, "No, Colonel, thank you, I never drink whiskey."

They rode a while longer, visiting pleasantly when the Colonel brought out some cigars from his pocket and said, "Mr. Lincoln, if you won't have a drink with me, won't you have a smoke with me?"

Mr. Lincoln said, "Colonel, you are a fine agreeable man to travel with, let me tell you a little story—an experience I had when I was a small boy. My mother called me to her bed when I was about nine years old. She was very sick and she said to me, 'Abbey, the doctor tells me I am not going to get well. Before I go I want you to promise me you will never use whiskey or tobacco as long as you live.' And I promised my mother I never would. Up to this hour I have kept that promise. Would you advise me to break my promise to my dear mother. . . .?"

ACTIVITY 58

RESPECTING MYSELF

58-1 I Have Purpose

Hold up a simple object such as a pencil, an eraser, a ruler, etc. Ask your students to identify what it is and the purpose for which it was made. Now ask, "Which is greater this object or the people who made it?" Point out that if something so simple as this object was created for a purpose, then each of them must have some purpose for being as well. Ask them to share some ideas on how they think people can find purpose in life through doing things that are helpful to others.

> **Discussion Opportunity:** Every person has a purpose for living, whether they know it or not. One of the primary goals every person should have is to discover that purpose. The key is that the purpose has to be larger than themselves. One good way to begin this process of discovery is to discover what your talents are and how to use these talents in the service of others as Florence Nightingale did. Those who limit their search to serving themselves will never fully live to their purpose. Character Traits: SR self-understanding, self-denial, self-reliance

58-2 There's More of Me to Find

As a class identify a service project in which the class can work together to help someone in need. After the project, discuss with the class how they felt when they were doing something useful to help others. Explain that sometimes in life, people have trouble finding themselves. Point out that when people are engaged in doing useful things to help others it is often easier to find themselves because there seems to be more of them to find.

Discussion Opportunity: No matter how talented and capable a person may be, a person is always more significant when those talents are used in the service of others. The greatness in Eleanor Roosevelt, Florence Nightingale, Abraham Lincoln, George Washington Carver, and Dr. Korczak lay not in their ability, but in how they chose to use that ability in making the world a better place. The same is true for each of us. Character Traits: SR self-understanding, self-denial, self-reliance; RO caring, citizenship

58-3   I have a Good Conscience

Both in public service and as a scientist, Benjamin Franklin often came under criticism by others. Following are comments Franklin made in letters to family and friends regarding some of these criticisms.

"My rule, in which I have always found satisfaction, is, never to turn aside in public affairs through views of private interest; but to go straight forward in doing what appears to be right at the time, leaving the consequences with Providence."

"I have long observed one rule. It is simply this—to be concerned in no affairs that I would blush to have made public."

"The internal satisfaction of a good conscience is always present, and time will do us justice in the minds of the people, even those at present the most prejudiced against us."

"One's true happiness depends more upon one's own judgment of one's own self. . . .than upon the applause of the unthinking, undiscerning multitude, who are apt to cry Hosanna today, and tomorrow, Crucify him."

Hindsight Questions
- What were two rules Franklin used to guide him?
- What did Franklin believe was necessary to achieve happiness?

Insight Questions
- How could Franklin's rules help him have a clear conscience?
- How can a clear conscience help a person be more happy?

Foresight Questions
- Why is a person who acts purely out of self-interest at risk of offending his or own conscience?
* Apart from being more happy, what are other advantages of having clear conscience?

58-4   Better Than I Found It

Challenge your class to find ways to leave people, places, and things better than they found them. Perhaps something's out of place and needs to be put away, something's broken they can fix, something's dirty they can clean, someone's hungry they can feed, etc. Have them begin by finding one specific thing and then reporting in class on what they did to make it better.

58-5 Sharing My Talents

Invite your students to identify ways in which they might use their talents to help other people and then do it. Have them individually share what they did and then discuss their experiences in class and how it made them feel.

58-6 Further Ahead Today Than Yesterday

Assign your students to keep a daily journal or log for a week. At the end of each day, have them list any progress they feel they made during the day in things they are trying to do. Entries may consist of things they learned, things they accomplished, decisions they have made, etc.

58-7 The Boy With a Smile

The boy with a smile was a friend indeed,
For he was a friend of those in need,
He saved a boy on the river Nile,
From the open jaws of a crocodile,
He shared his lunch of fried, dried boar,
With a hungry child who was mighty poor,
He gave some water to a thirsty man,
Lost in the desert of the vast Sudan,
He brought a blanket to stop the chill,
Of a poor old woman who was feeling ill,
He was helping others all the while,
And that's why the boy wore a great big smile.

58-8 The Girl With a Grin

The girl with the grin was mighty good,
For she was a girl who understood,
To her work was a pleasure and not a chore,
Learning was fun and not a bore,
The way she learned most any skill
Was plenty of practice with lots of drill,
She made the most of every day,
And still had time for work and play,
She said others might help but you must do,
They may cheer but it's up to you,
So she was up in the morning and soon dug in,
That's why the girl wore a great big grin.

Discussion Opportunity: Self-Respect is earned, not bestowed. It comes from within, not without. Moreover some activities are activities more likely to create self-respect than others. Having a clear conscience and good habits are two. Another is to be engaged in doing good to others. The key is in doing your best each day with what you have to make the world a little better place. The act may be as simple as picking up a loose piece of paper or as grand as finding a cure for a disease. But both, in their own way make the world a little better. No useful act is ever wasted. No kind or considerate act is ever wasted. The rewards may not always immediate or easily recognized. But if you patiently persist in doing good things—someone, somewhere will be the better for it and so will you. Character Traits: SR self-understanding, self-reliance, RO caring, citizenship

CHOOSING TO RESPECT OTHERS

Section Five

LEARNING OBJECTIVES FOR SECTION FIVE

Appreciates three ways in which we show our respect for others

    Caring

    Fairness

    Honoring

Recognize that all people have common needs

Understands how individual differences help us meet common needs

SECTION OVERVIEW

The scriptural injunction, "Therefore all things whatsoever ye would that others should do to you, do ye even so to them" is by far the best guide to mutual respect ever given. Known as the Golden Rule, it has been endorsed by philosophers of all ages. But for all its merit, the Golden Rule is not the general rule, and as the words of a song remind us, "Hate is strong and mocks the song of Peace on Earth Good Will to Men."

There are many causes for the lack of mutual respect, but none that aren't related to personal choices people make. Some have to do with differences in religious, political, or philosophical beliefs. Some have to do with differences in racial or ethnic origin. Other causes of disrespect arise out of pure selfishness, unleashing the purple passions of greed and lust. Not infrequently, the inability to respect others arises from a lack of self-respect. Sometimes, simple misunderstandings unleash torrents of hate and revenge. But whatever the cause, when such feelings arise, the Golden Rule goes out the door and people do things to others they would never in a hundred years want to have done to themselves. Whether manifested in rudeness and incivility or in pogroms for exterminating ethnic minorities, lack of respect for others is a plague that robs the human family of both peace and prosperity.

Three important ways in which respect may be manifest are caring, fairness, and honoring.

Caring

When we truly care about others, we will more likely treat them respectfully. While it is far easier to care for others when we feel they care for us, becoming a caring person is something we can choose to do independently of what anyone else does.

Fairness

A commitment to play by the rules, to treat others impartially, and to be just in our relations with others is another way in which we manifest respect for others. Caring is a pre-requisite to fairness. Only caring people will choose to be fair in dealing with others.

Honoring

Honoring the personal and property rights of others is perhaps the highest manifestation of respect. Caring and Fairness are prerequisites to Honoring. Honoring is the basic objective of the U.S. Constitution and is the foundation on which civilization rests.

For children to grasp these ideas and be meaningful to them they must understand two fundamental things.
1) That every living person has the same basic needs and in this respect we are all created equal, and
2) That individual differences are essential to our mutual well-being, for it is these very differences that enable us to meet our common needs and that provide the interest and variety so necessary to life.

ACTIVITY 59

THE LANGUAGE OF RESPECT
Synonyms and Antonyms

On the board, write the words listed in the left column and the column headings "Synomyms" and "Antonyms" across the top. Ask your students to give you words that mean the same thing as the words in the left column and write them under synonyms. Then, have them give you words that have the opposite meaning of the words in th left column and write them in the right column under antonyms.

	Synonyms	Antonyms
Care, caring	carefulness, concern, regard	careless, disregard, unconcern
Kind,	good-hearted, gentle,	cruel, mean, harsh
Honor	esteem, regard	scorn, contempt
Civil	courteous, mannerly, polite	discourteous, rude, ill-mannered
Considerate	thoughtful, kind, sympathetic	inconsiderate, unkind, unthoughtful

Next, have your students give you examples of things people say and do that would be representative of different words on the board and discuss how these represent the differences between respectful and disrespectful behavior.

ACTIVITY 60

DIFFERENCES ACTIVITIES

Use the following activities to demonstrate how individual differences are necessary for our mutual well-being. Important points to consider include how individual differences add variety and interest to life. Think how boring life would be if everyone were exactly alike. Since no one knows everything or even clearly understands everything they know, different viewpoints are necessary to help us increase our knowledge and understanding. Each of has different talents which make it possible to meet our different needs. No one can do everything and everyone can do something. Different sizes, shapes, and color help us tell each other apart and add variety. It is our differences that make it possible to meet our common needs.

60-1　　　　How Differences Help Meet Common Needs

With your students, brainstorm two lists: 1) ways in which people are different from each other and, 2) needs which all people have in common. List these on the board. Together identify ways in which the proper use of these differences can better help everyone to meet their common needs.

60-2   Betty One-Note

ADVANCE PREPARATION: *In advance of class, prepare a cassette tape containing a demonstration of Betty One-Note's music (ie. one note repeated over and over) and a few brief selections from various kinds of music; instrumental, vocal, classical, popular, rock, etc. Try to include some music from different cultures. In class read and discuss Betty One-Note:*

Once upon a time, there was a young girl named Betty One-Note. Betty loved to play the piano. Betty especially liked to play middle C. She liked the sound of middle C so much better than any other note on the piano that middle C was the only note Betty ever played. For hours at a time, Betty would sit at the piano playing middle C over and over again, at the same tempo, and at the same volume.

Play cassette tape of Betty One-Note playing her one note or demonstrate on a musical instrument.

Ask and discuss:
- What do you think others thought of Betty's music?
- What would the world be like if there were only one note? Only one song? Only one musical instrument?
- How are people like musical tones or sounds?

Now play different musical selections from the tape. Discuss the importance of musicians working together to achieve balance in harmony, volume, and tempo. Explore the beauty, interest, and richness of the different variations in musical form.

60-3   The Hammer and the Saw

Read the following story starter about the hammer and the saw to your students. Either individually or in small groups, assign them to create a story or skit about how the hammer and the saw discover how they can accomplish far more working together to achieve common goals than either one could ever do alone.

One day, said the hammer to the saw, "What good are you?
You're so flat and skinny, there's nothing you can do.
And with your jagged edges, you're a sorry sight to see.
So go away, anywhere, just far away from me."

"Well!" said the saw, "Who needs the likes of you!
I'll gladly leave you here to do whatever hammers do.
It's plain enough to see we're not at all alike,
And there's nothing much in you I could ever find to like."

Ask and discuss:
- What do a hammer and a saw have in common?
- How do the differences between a hammer and a saw make them more useful than if they were exactly alike?
- How are a hammer and a saw like people?

ACTIVITY 61

LIKENESS ACTIVITIES

Use one or more of the following activities to demonstrate ways in which all people are alike. After the activity, discuss how every living person has essentially the same need for food, water, rest, shelter, transportation, love, education, and opportunity. Explore how all people have thoughts and feelings, experience joy and sadness, and have talents and skills they can contribute to the mutual good. Point out that when we talk about "all men being created equal" in the Declaration of Independence, we are talking about the ways in which we are all alike. That is what being equal means. Follow the activity and discussion with one of the empathy activities on page 131.

61-1   Likeness Writing Project

ADVANCE PREPARATION: *Obtain from "National Geographic" or other sources, pictures of from different cultures. As a class identify different ways in which the children in these pictures are alike. Then have your students write a paper on how these likeness create common needs and give common purpose to all people. Discuss their papers and the HIF questions below.*

61-2   Cultural Likeness Research Project

Divide your class into small groups. Assign each group one of the following categories of human need: food, clothing, housing, transportation, education, work, or recreation. Ask each group to identify how people in different cultures meet the need assigned to them, then present their findings to the rest of the class. After the activity, discuss the HIF questions below.

61-3   Needs All People Have Puzzle

ADVANCE PREPARATION: *Prepare copies of the puzzle activity on page 133.*
Have your students complete the activity and then discuss the following questions.

Hindsight Questions
- What are some needs all people have in common?

Insight Questions
- Why may these be considered needs?
- How do these needs make us equal?
- Why is it important to recognize ways in which all people are equal?

Foresight Questions:
- What happens when we are careless in taking care of our needs?
- What happens when we disregard the importance of needs others have?

Discussion Opportunities: All people are created equal in that they have the same or similar needs. One of the legitimate purposes of government is to assure its citizens have the freedom, resources, and opportunities to fill these needs without injury to others. A mark of good citizenship is honoring the laws that provide these protections and honoring the rights and property of others. Character Traits: RO caring, fairness, citizenship

ACTIVITY 62

EMPATHY ACTIVITIES

62-1 Blindfolded Art Project

Have your students close their eyes. With their eyes closed, assign them to take out of their desk a pencil, some crayons, and a piece of paper. Have them draw and color a picture with their eyes closed. Because it is difficult for many children to keep their eyes closed, it would be an advantage to have blindfolds if possible. Discuss the HIF questions below.

62-2 One Handed Activity

Have each student place their best hand (ie. the right hand if right handed) behind their back and perform one of the following activities with their remaining hand. Discuss the HIF questions below.
1. *Shape a specific object from modeling clay.*
2. *Fold a piece of paper and cut out paper dolls.*
3. *Assemble an object or lace and tie a shoe.*

62-3 No Handed Art Project

Have your students draw a picture or write a story holding a pencil, crayons, or paints:
1. *In their mouth*
2. *With their toes*

Hindsight Questions
- How difficult was this activity?

Insight Questions
- How does the loss of the use of one or more parts of your body make life more difficult?
- How would you like others to treat you if you were disabled in this way?
- What would be required of you or another person to overcome or work around this disability?

Foresight Questions
- Why is it important for you to appreciate the needs of others?

62-4   A Meal At Ravensbruk

This activity may be used with "Return from Ravensbruk" p. 134

ADVANCE PREPARATION: *Prepare a thin turnip soup made simply from boiling one or two turnips, without seasoning, in a large pot of water until the turnips become mushy and dissolve in the water. Serve with a slice of black bread. Also required are paper bowls and plastic spoons. Alternatively, just serve a slice of black bread to eat and a glass of water.*

During World War Two, one of the goals of the Nazi government was to exterminate all Jews and other ethnic minorities in Europe. This goal was implemented in several ways. One method of extermination was to place prisoners in forced labor camps where they would be worked as slaves and fed a starvation diet. Ravensbruk, Germany was the location of an extermination camp for women. The diet for prisoners at Ravensbruk consisted of a slice of black bread for breakfast, and a ladle of thin turnip soup for dinner. Sometimes the soup would be accompanied by a small boiled potato.

Hindsight Questions
- How would you like to live on this diet?

Insight Questions
- Why is it unjust to deprive others of food and the necessities of life?
- Why were some of the ways the Nazi's were disrespectful of others?

Foresight Questions
- Why is it important to make sure we always honor the personal and property rights of others?

Needs All People Have

Using the clues below, circle the hidden words and fill in the blanks by each clue.
Find words by by reading words forward, backward, up, down, or diagonally.

```
Z  G  K  N  O  W  L  E  D  G  E  P
S  G  A  S  K  M  S  V  T  N  X  R
H  R  T  V  L  R  N  F  H  I  K  R
E  O  X  Y  G  E  N  R  S  P  E  M
L  Z  X  E  Y  T  E  G  A  T  W  J
T  B  N  I  P  A  E  P  L  E  A  P
E  U  O  A  N  W  K  E  S  T  T  D
R  C  D  P  X  U  H  L  A  U  E  V
R  O  O  E  P  S  Z  K  F  C  R  E
C  L  O  E  X  E  R  C  I  S  E  R
I  M  F  E  D  U  D  I  T  R  S  A
```

1. You breathe in, plants give off _O_ __ __ __ __ __

   Why is this a need?_____

2. Your main source of energy. _F_ __ __ __

   Why is this a need?_____

3. You usually do this at night. _S_ __ __ __ __

   Why is this a need?_____

4. Your body mostly consists of. _W_ __ __ __ __

   Why is this a need?_____

5. A place protect you from the weather. _S_ __ __ __ __ __ __

   Why is this a need?_____

6. Your muscles need to get _E_ __ __ __ __ __ __ __

   Why is this a need?_____

7. The reason you go to school. _K_ __ __ __ __ __ __ __ __

   Why is this a need?_____

BIOGRAPHY

ACTIVITY 63

RETURN FROM RAVENSBRUK

As the train jerked and bumped along the damaged track, a frail, elderly lady sat next to the window looking out. Tears came to her eyes to see the once beautiful Germany pass before her, now a wasteland of villages reduced to rubble, fire blackened woods, wrecked and twisted vehicles along the roads, and worst of all, women and children wandering and scrounging to find food and shelter. She herself, was faint from lack of food. She hadn't eaten for over two days. The trip had seemed endless. Often the train traveled at a crawl. Some sections of track were entirely gone and there had been long detours and frequent changes in trains. But now, she was near the Dutch border. Every mile took her closer to home.

Corrie leaned back and closed her eyes. Hopefully, the nightmare was over. But Corrie was not sure what she would find when she got back home.

"How long has it been?" Corrie asked herself, "Let's see. It was February 28, 1944 when they took us away. Today is January 3, 1945. Is that possible? Only ten months? It seems like forever!"

Corrie thought back, before this terrible war had begun. Life was very secure and pleasant for her and her family. She and her sister, Betsie lived comfortably with their father, a watchmaker in Haarlem, Netherlands. Her father was in his eighties and she and Betsie were both in their fifties. Her father was known as the "Grand old man of Haarlem." The family had lived in the same house for well over a hundred years. Her brother Wilhelm and her sister Nollie lived with their families near by. They lived peaceably with their neighbors, and all in all, it was a very happy existence. But, the war had suddenly changed all of that.

She remembered the day Germany invaded Holland. It seemed like a dream. The explosions, the bright flashes in the sky, the announcement of surrender five days later, and the arrival of German troops to occupy their city.

For a while, things did not seem much different, but then it began, just little things at first, hard to recognize as persecution. A rock through the window of a Jewish-owned store. Ugly words scrawled on the wall of the synagogue. Then signs in windows of certain restaurants and stores, "Jews will not be served here." Then all Jews were required to wear bright yellow stars sewn to their clothes. Corrie remembered how surprised she was to learn how many of her neighbors were Jewish. At first the Germans were testing the Dutch people to see what their reaction would be. She remembered how ashamed she had been to learn how many of her countrymen were not only tolerating such treatment of people who had been their neighbors for years, but how many were actually participating.

Before long, Jews were not allowed in theaters, museums, and even libraries. There were arrests. People began disappearing. Stores were broken into and looted by German soldiers. People were thrown out of their homes so others could occupy them. Then finally began the systematic roundup and deportation of Jews to concentration camps.

Corrie thought about that first night, when her father had invited Mrs. Kleermaker to stay with them. It was in May of 1942. Mr. Kleermaker had been imprisoned and the Gestapo had ordered her to close the family clothing store. She was afraid to go back to her apartment and had come to Corrie's father for help. Soon, there were two other guests, all equally afraid to return home. It was then that Corrie and her family realized they must do something to help these people get away from Haarlem. Almost overnight, Corrie, Betsie, and their elderly father became the center of a major, systematic, underground effort to rescue Jews and to get them out of Holland before the Germans found them. Within weeks, a secret hiding room had been built in their house, and they were involved in obtaining false passports, stolen rationing cards, and sending secret messages. Corrie and her family had known from the beginning that the Germans would likely catch up with them, and their race to get as many Jews out of Holland as possible would be over.

In February, Corrie, Betsie, and their father were arrested and imprisoned. It was several months later that she learned her father had only lived about ten days. She remembered with pride how, when offered immunity if he promised not to cause anymore trouble, her father had stood erect and with quiet dignity informed the interrogator that if released, he would open his door to any person in need who knocked.

She and Betsie were imprisoned near Amsterdam until August when they were transported to Germany. She thought back on the train ride to Germany. As bad as this trip in returning back to Holland was, it was nothing compared to her trip to Germany. Along with hundreds of other women, Betsie and Corrie had been herded into railroad boxcars. They were packed so tightly they couldn't sit. The heat in the boxcars was searing, and there were no provisions for water or sanitary facilities. The stench, the thirst, the suffering were almost unbearable.

Only the misery of the trip had made their arrival at Ravensbruk seem welcome. Ravensbruk, the notorious women's extermination camp was not designed for the least degree of comfort. The women were required to sleep on great, square platforms, three tiers high and nine persons on each tier. The rancid straw, the backed up plumbing, the lice, the filth, all combined to make the barracks a most unpleasant place to live.

It did not take long to discover what life at Ravensbruk would be like, forced labor each day, living in filthy barracks, and fed on a slice of black bread for breakfast and thin turnip soup for lunch and dinner with an occasional boiled potato. Under these circumstances, many women did not live long. Already reduced to skin and bones from a sparse prison diet, Corrie and Betsie, were not in very good condition when they arrived. In December, Betsie died. It still amazed Corrie to reflect upon Betsie's faith and goodness, and how even in these dismal circumstances she had found it within herself to feel sorry for the brutal German, to find ways to help others in the camp, and to retain her faith in the goodness of both God and man. Yet she had, and through her, so had Corrie.

The train shuddered to a stop. Corrie looked up. This was the end of the line, Groningen.

"I'm in Holland! I'm almost home!" The thoughts shot through her mind and spread joy to every bone of her body. But as she stood to leave the train, Corrie realized how weak she was. It took every thing she had, but somehow she managed to get off the train and to find her way to the local hospital. Once inside, a kindly nurse led her into a room where she explained her story. The nurse left and was soon back with a tray of tea and some crisp bread.

"You're suffering from malnutrition." the nurse gently explained, "You must be careful what you eat. While you eat this, I'll draw you a hot tub of water."

It had been so long since anyone had treated Corrie with kindness, the nurse's offer brought tears of gratitude to her eyes.

Hindsight Questions
- What were Corrie's feelings as she looked at the wrecked villages and people scrounging for food?
* Why were Corrie and Betsie sent to Ravensbruk?

Insight Questions
- What motives do you think might cause some people to treat other people so cruelly?
- What did it take for Corrie and her family to decide to take Jewish refugees into their home?

Foresight Questions
- How might this story illustrate the statement that respect and disrespect are like boomerangs?
- Between Corrie and her captors, who do you think could feel best about what they had done?

Discussion Opportunity: All people have similar needs. Attempts to deprive other people of their rights to meet these needs are destructive to both aggressor and victim. Aggressors create enemies who frequently repay in kind, plus they lose all claim to internal peace of mind and self-respect. Character Traits: RO caring, fairness, citizenship

ACTIVITY 64

RULES ACTIVITIES

64-1   The School Without Rules

Assign your students to write a brief one page story about attending a school in which there are no rules. A school in which students, teachers, custodians, principals, and everyone else does just what they want, when they want. What would such a school be like?

Invite several of your students to read their stories and discuss how rules bring order to life.

64-2   Rules We Live By

On the board, write in three column headings, "Rules", "Who Makes", and "Why" Under the heading "Rules" write "Home", "School", and "Government." Have your students identify and then list three or four rules in each of these categories they are required to obey. Now fill in the second and third column for each of these categories identifying who makes each of these rules, and why they made these rules. Explore with your students why voluntary submission to proper authority is essential to individual and collective well-being.

64-3   Anarchy and Tyranny

Have your students write two column headings on a piece of paper, "Anarchy" and "Tyranny." Read the words below and have them write the word in the column they think it belongs. Explain the difference between Anarchy and Tyranny and discuss how Tyranny represents the abuse of authority and Anarchy represents a failure to respect proper authority.

Mob rule, despotism, domineering, chaos, confusion, oppression, disorder, lawlessness, no freedom, dictatorship, no rules, slave.

Discussion Opportunity: Tyranny or oppression exis when people abuse their authority. Examples of this are slavery and Nazi Germany during WWII. When people choose not to obey legitimate laws or authority, anarchy exits. An example of anarchy is mob rule. Safety lies in having just laws, voluntary obedience to those laws, and someone authorized to enforce them when people chooseß not to obey them. Character Traits: PR duty, ownership; SR self-denial; RO caring, citizenship

ACTIVITY 65

RETURN FROM VIETNAM

Author Unknown

The Creightons were very proud of their son Frank. When he went to college, naturally they missed him; but he wrote and they looked forward to his letters and saw him on weekends. Then Frank was drafted into the army.

After he had been in the army about five months, he was sent to Vietnam. Of course, their anxiety for Frank was greater than ever before. Every week they heard from him they were thankful for his well-being. Then one week went by without a letter—two weeks—and finally three. At the end of the third week a telegram came, saying, "We regret to inform you that your son has been missing for three weeks and is presumed to have been killed in action while fighting for his country."

The parents were heart stricken. They tried to accept the situation and go on living, but they missed Frank terribly.

About three weeks later, the phone rang. When Mrs. Creighton answered it, a voice on the other end said, "Mother, it's Frank. They found me, and I'm going to be all right. I'm in the United States and I'm coming home soon."

Mrs. Creighton was overjoyed. She sobbed, "Oh, that's wonderful! That's just wonderful, Frank."

There was silence for a moment, and then Frank said, "Mother I want to ask you something that is important to me. While I've been here, I've met a lot of wonderful people and I've really become close friends with some. There is one fellow I would like to bring home with me to meet you and Dad. I would like to know if it would be all right if he could stay and live with us, because he has no place else to go."

His mother assured him it would be all right.

Then Frank said, "You see, he wasn't as lucky as some; he was injured in battle. He was hit by a blast and his face is disfigured. He lost his leg, and his right hand is missing. So you see, he feels uneasy about how others will accept him."

Frank's mother stopped to think a minute. She began to wonder how things would work out, and what people in town would think of someone like that. She said, "Sure Frank, you bring him home—for a visit, that is. We would love to meet him and have him stay for a while; but about his staying with us permanently, well, we'll have to think about that." There was silence for a minute, and then Frank said, "Okay, Mother." and hung up.

A week went by without any word from Frank, and then a telegram arrived—"We regret to inform you that your son has taken his life. We would like you to come and identify the body."

Their son was gone. The sorrow stricken parents could only ask, "Why had he done this?" When they walked into the room to identify their son's body, they found a young man with a disfigured face, one leg missing, and his right hand gone.

Hindsight Questions
- What did Frank ask his parents?

Insight Questions
- Why did Frank ask them that question?

•Foresight Questions
- How do you think the Creightons felt about their answer to Frank's question?

ACTIVITY 66

HE STOLE MY LUNCH

Author Unknown

Mr. Kames greeted the students as they came into the school house. He knew this may well be the most challenging day of his life. He had accepted the teaching position of this little one room school in the back woods of Virginia knowing full well the problem he was facing. The last three teachers had been driven away by the rowdiness of the boys. They seemed to delight in tormenting every teacher they had. It was as if they dared anyone to teach them anything. This was Mr. Kames first school. It was his first day of teaching. What was he going to do?

As the students came into the school, Mr. Kames overheard Tom, the biggest boy in the class say, "I can handle this teacher all by myself."

Mr. Kames decided the best thing to do would be to establish some very strict rules, right up front, but he decided to see if he could get the students to suggest and agree upon what the rules should be.

With some effort, Mr. Kames succeeded in getting the students settled down long enough to say, "This is my first school to ever teach. In fact this is my first day of teaching. I want us to learn together, but I need your help. First of all, we need some rules. Can you suggest some?"

"No stealing!" shouted Jason.

"Can't be late!" said Mary.

One by one, different rules were suggested until Mr. Kames had written ten on the black board.

"Now," said Mr. Kames, "We have some rules. But we also need some kind of punishment if anyone doesn't follow the rules."

"Ten hard swats on the back with a switch and without a coat on." suggested Tom.

"That seems rather harsh to me," responded Mr. Kames, "wouldn't it be better to choose something a little milder?"

"No! That's what we want." chimed in most of the boys as if they anticipated some delight in seeing who would be first to get a switching.

Fortunately, the school went along pretty well for the first three days. Then arose the first problem. Tom's lunch had been stolen.

"Who ever stole it," declared Tom, "better get a good switching."

Mr. Kames soon discovered the culprit, a skinny little eight year old named Jim. Jim was a rather quiet boy, who more or less kept to himself.

"He's got to be switched." said Tom. The other boys all agreed.

Mr. Kames was troubled. "How can I switch this boy?" he asked himself, "But, how can I not?"

Jim came forward to be switched, a small child even in his coat.

"Please," said Jim, "don't make me take my coat off."

"I don't have any choice, Jim," said Mr. Kames with his heart in his throat, "that's the rule everyone agreed to."

Reluctantly, Jim removed his coat. Every one was startled to see that he did not have a shirt on. There was only his thin, bony body underneath the coat. It was obvious he did not get much to eat.

"Why don't you have a shirt on, Jim?" Mr. Kames gently asked.

Tearfully, Jim explained, "My father died two years ago. Me and my mother, we're pretty poor. We don't have any money right now. I know I shouldn't have taken Tom's lunch, but I was so dreadfully hungry, I did it anyway."

There was silence for a few minutes as what Jim had said sank in. Suddenly, Tom stepped to the front of the class. Removing his coat, he said,

"I'll take the switching for Jim."

Hindsight Questions
- Why did Mr. Kames want the students to establish their own rules?

Insight Questions
- Why was it important for Mr. Kames class to have rules?
- Why did Mr. Kames feel obligated to go ahead with the switching?
- Why did Tom volunteer to take the switching for Tom?

Foresight Questions
- Why are rules and laws necessary in families, schools, and communities?

Discussion Opportunity: Mr. Kames knew that for learning to take place in his classroom, there had to be order. He also knew that students would more readily obey rules they had some ownership in. The students all knew that when the rules were in place they had to follow them. What they didn't foresee was the special needs of one of their members. No one took greater ownership of the rule of switching than did Tom in offering to take the switching for Jim. Tom had been a major instigator in getting the rule established and in pressing that it should be applied to the person who stole his lunch. But, perhaps for the first time in his life, Tom experienced empathy and cared more for someone else's feelings than he did for his own. Character Traits: PR ownership, SR self-denial RO caring, citizenship

ACTIVITY 67

RESPECT IS LIKE

As a class, or in small groups, brainstorm answers to the following two statements: "Respect is like. . . ." and "Disrespect is like . . . ." Require your students to explain why they think the examples they have chosen are like the one or the other. Some examples might be:

- Respect and disrespect are like boomerangs. How you treat others will come back to you.
- Respect is like motor oil. With oil, there is little or no friction and the motor will run well for a long time. Without the oil, friction will over heat the motor and it will quit running. Disrespect is like running a motor without oil.
- Disrespect is like pathogenic bacteria that causes illnesses like tuberculosis, cholera, and malaria. Respect is like the helpful bacteria that are used in making many important food household products.
- Respect is like a fire in the fire place. It warms and cheers those who are near. Disrespect is like a raging fire that's out of control. It burns, and destroys everything it comes in contact with.
- Respect is like a gentle rain bringing badly needed moisture so crops and plants can grow. Disrespect is like a torrential rain that floods and destroys everything that's in its way.

Discussion Opportunity: Nearly everyone has some idea of what respect and disrespect are like, especially when it applies to how others treat them. They know it by how they feel when people treat them respectfully or disrespectfully. But knowing is not enough. Treating others respectfully must be a conscious choice followed by a committed effort or it won't happen. All that is needed is for Passionata to make you upset or Perverter to unloose a Puff Prejudge befogger on you and you will say or do unkind things as if you never knew the difference. To avoid falling under their influence you need strong C skills. Character Traits: PR ownership; RO caring, fairness, citizenship

BIOGRAPHY

HARRIET BEGINS "UNCLE TOM'S CABIN"

Harriet finished writing and looked up with relief. The anguish of indecision and doubt that had plagued Harriet for the past several months were now dissolved. She felt a calm and quiet resolve. It would take several months and would be difficult, but now she knew what to do and actually believed she could do it.

Harriet reflected upon the events that had brought her to this point. For months, she had frequently lain awake at night, distressed, frustrated, and troubled. Harriet had long been opposed to slavery and with the passing of the Fugitive Slave Act of 1850, every fibre of her being strained to speak out against the evils of human bondage and the unjustness of this law.

But what could she say that would make any difference? Was it right for a woman to write against slavery? Where would she, a mother with six children to care for, get the time? What perils might she be subjecting her family to? Was it true, as some people suggested, that it was unpatriotic and seditious to write and speak against slavery? These and a thousand other questions had continually troubled Harriet. But now, it all seemed clear to her. She still did not have the whole story worked out in her mind, but she was sure she had just finished writing the ending to the story.

Harriet wanted to paint a picture with words that would show in its full ugly hue, the degrading influence of slavery on both slaves and slave holders. It was her intent to capture the suffering of mothers whose children had been torn from them; of men, women, and children forced into back breaking labor, often without adequate food, clothing, or housing; of people deprived of protection from the law and and whipped into obedience by the lash. She also wanted to show the dehumanizing influence of slavery on the slave holders and it's destructive influence on them and their families. But, Harriet also wanted

to show the love, the faith, and the exceptional moral character of many of those who were slaves. It would be a novel based on the real life experiences of individuals about whom she had some personal knowledge.

It would include the thrilling story of Eliza Harris who ran away from her master when she discovered that she and her child were to be sold to different buyers. Eliza had fled with her child from a plantation in Kentucky to the Ohio river in hopes the river was still frozen. Unfortunately, a thaw had set in and the ice was broken into large floating chunks. As her pursuers began to close in on her with a pack of dogs, Eliza decided to either cross the river or die in the attempt. With her child in her arms, she jumped, slipped, and scrambled from one ice chunk to another. A man watching from the Ohio side was deeply moved by Eliza's courage and helped her to safety.

Harriet would include the story of James Birney, a slave holder from Kentucky who freed his slaves and became an active opponent of slavery. Also, she was sure she wanted to include the story of John Van Zandt, who lost his farm and possessions for assisting fugitive slaves. Then of course, there were the multitude of stories that had been told to her by fugitive slaves she and her husband Calvin had known and helped. Surely, she had enough material to work from.

Of all the stories she had heard of slavery, however, none haunted her more than a story she had first read many years before in a book titled, *Slavery As It Is*, by Theodore Weld. It was the true story of a slave owner and his neighbor who had a dispute about the religious convictions of slaves. The neighbor argued that slaves only pretended to believe in God, but deep down inside were just hypocrites. The slave owner countered by saying that he had a slave he was sure would be willing to die rather than deny his beliefs. The neighbor doubted the owner so they decided to put it to the test. The owner had the slave brought to them and ordered him to deny his religious beliefs. The slave, Tom, would not obey his master, so the owner had Tom put to the lash. As Tom was being mercilessly whipped, the owner kept promising Tom that any time he denied his faith he would be freed. After two hundred lashes, the slave died.

Now, in front of Harriet lay the story she had just written. It told of another Tom, a slave who was lashed until he died for refusing to tell his master the whereabouts of two run away slave girls. It was a compelling ending and one that gave full force to Harriet's feelings about the cruelty and injustice of slavery. Now, with the ending in mind, Harriett Beecher Stowe had finally begun to write her story of Uncle Tom's Cabin.

Hindsight Questions
- What obstacles did Harriet have to overcome in writing *Uncle Tom's Cabin*?
- What was Harriet's motivation for writing the book?

Insight Questions
- What was wrong with slavery?
- How did slavery violate the principle that all men are created equal?
- What types of Error-Prone thinking are used to justify slavery?

Foresight Questions
- What would America be like today if slavery had continued?

Discussion Opportunity: The vicious effects of EPT are no where more evident than in instances of class hatred or oppression. Abraham Lincoln said he often wished, when he heard someone extol the virtues of slavery, that if they thought it such a good thing they would try it themselves. Perverter is the author of thinking that exaggerates the rights of one class of citizens while minimizing or ignoring the rights of another class of citizens. Prevaricator creates the lies that justify this kind of thinking, Possessit provides the motivation, and Passionata the emotional energy to act on it. But whenever such thinking prevails, it is mutually destructive. The slave owner who whipped Tom till he died perhaps lost more than Tom. Character Traits: PR right, ownership; SR self-understanding, self-denial; RO caring, fairness, citizenship; T honesty

---

BIOGRAPHY

ACTIVITY 69

LUNATICS DON'T FEEL THE COLD

A Biographical Sketch of Dorthea Dix Written in First Person

It has been said of me that, during my lifetime, I was one of the most influential women in America. I don't know about that. I doubt that you have ever even heard my name and probably know little about the work to which I devoted my life. That of itself is of no consequence. I share my story with you to encourage you to believe that one person, even of little means, can do much good in the world if he or she is willing.

My first career was in teaching. I started my own schools in which I taught. I started my first school when I was fourteen and sometimes had as many as twenty students attending my classes. My second career, however, is the one of most interest. At the age of thirty-six, I inherited a small bequest from my grandmother. It relieved me from the necessity of continuing to work, and after having taught for over twenty years, I wanted a more leisurely life, but such was not to be.

After retiring, I settled in Massachusetts to enjoy what I anticipated would be a comfortable and uncomplicated life. Then, one day I volunteered to teach a Sunday School class in the East Cambridge jail. After giving my little class, I decided to visit with some of the prisoners. While roaming through the jail, I came upon a section reserved for lunatic women. The conditions were appalling. The room was filthy. The women were deprived of even the most basic comforts of cleanliness. The room did not have any heat and was miserably cold. When I raised my concerns to the jailer, he said that lunatics don't feel the cold. I was enraged. I called the situation to the attention of a number of prominent citizens in the city and, with their help, conditions at the jail were greatly improved for these poor women.

This, however, was not the end for me but rather the beginning. I began wondering how many other unfortunate beings were in similar conditions. I took it upon myself, at my own expense, to visit other jails and almshouses to see what conditions for these people really were. I was terribly distressed to find that the conditions at East Cambridge jail were pretty common for people with serious mental problems.

Within twelve miles of Boston, I found human beings labeled as lunatics who were confined in cages, closets, cellars, stalls, and pens. They were often chained, naked, and beaten with rods or lashed with whips. With the information I collected, I submitted a memorial to the state legislature. It began, "I come to present the strong claim of suffering humanity. . . ."

You can imagine my surprise when my memorial was met with a storm of opposition. I discovered that society is often offended when confronted with unpleasant truths that reflect poorly upon its self-righteousness. Some people said I didn't know what I was talking about. Some said I was meddling in things that were not my business. Still others tried to brand me as a trouble maker and said I was irresponsible in submitting my memorial. This opposition merely strengthened my resolve. The next forty years of my life were spent in trying to relieve the suffering of these poor, unhappy souls. In that time, I crissed-crossed the United States from one end to the other and traveled in most of the countries of the world. Every place I went I inspected jails, hospitals, and almshouses. I crusaded for improvements in the care of the insane.

In my crusade, I corresponded with Presidents and Kings, and with Ministers and Doctors, with anyone who might have influence to initiate the changes that were so badly needed. Many generous and noble individuals came to my aid and at the end of the forty years, when I could no longer continue, I could say we had made much progress. Great improvements had taken place in the quality of both the facilities and the care of mentally disturbed individuals, all over the world. I was grateful to have played a part in making these necessary changes.

Perhaps, one of the greatest compliments given me, was written by Dr. Charles Folsom in his book, *Diseases of the Mind*, in which he said,

"Her frequent visits to our institutions of the insane, and her searching criticisms, represent a better lunacy commission that would likely be appointed in many of our states."

For his kindness, I was grateful. But, to me, the greatest reward was in knowing that somehow, I had made a difference in a few lives, not the least of which was my own.

Hindsight Questions
- What experience changed the direction of Dorthea's life?
- What kind of difficulties did Dorthea run into in her efforts to help people with mental illnesses?

Insight Questions
- In what respect was Dorthea different from the jailer she talked to?
- Why do you think Dorthea was enraged at the jailer's response that lunatic's can't feel the cold?
- Why do you think some people resisted her efforts to help the mentally ill?
- What do you think motivated Dorthea to do what she did?

Foresight Questions
- How do you think Dorthea might have felt toward the end of her life about what she had done?

Discussion Opportunity: Dorthea had empathy for the suffering of the poor women in the jail. This empathy gave her the capacity to care about them and their feelings. She felt they were being treated unfairly, and even cruelly. Criticism allowed her to question the practices then prevailing in the care of mentally ill patients. Curiosity motivated her to find out how extensive the problem was. Creativity, Concentration, and Communication enabled her to become an effective advocate in their behalf and brought about major Corrections in the thinking of other people about the kind of care that should be provided these people. Dorthea required these C skills in combatting the EPT she frequently encountered. All too many allowed themselves to become prejudiced against the mentally ill and to exaggerate the difficulties of providing adequate care for them while minimizing the need for providing it. Character Traits: PR ownership; SR self-denial, self-reliance; RO caring, fairness, citizenship

---

BIOGRAPHY

JULY 13

The two men faced each other; Dr. Puetz, with his whip in one hand and a pistol at his side; Fritz Graebe, tired, drawn, and with an automatic weapon in his hand. Behind Dr. Puetz were several hundred emaciated men squatted on the ground, surrounded by the SS troops and Ukraine Militiamen who were guarding them.

The confrontation was a direct result of the policy of Jewish extermination undertaken by the Nazi government during WWII. The justification for this policy was outlined on July 13, 1941 by Henrich Himmler. Addressing SS troops about to leave for the Russian front, Himmler encouraged the troops to do their duty by explaining to them:

"This is an ideological battle and a struggle of races. Here in this struggle stands National Socialism: an ideology based on the value of our Germanic, Nordic blood. Here stands a world as we have conceived it: . . . .a happy, beautiful world full of culture: this is what our Germany is like. On the other side stands a population of 180 millions, a mixture of races, whose very names are unpronounceable, and whose physique is such that one can shoot them down without pity and compassion. These animals. . . .have been welded by the Jews into one religion, one ideology, that is called Bolshevism. . . ."

Himmler, head of the SS storm troopers was given particular responsibility by Hitler for eliminating all Jews in Europe. As as result, the SS in every country which had fallen to the German armies, was conducting systematic programs of mass murder for the intent of exterminating first the Jews, to be followed by Gypsies, Poles, and eventually all other "subhuman" races identified by Hitler and his cronies. Now, one year to the day later, this policy was being acted out in a dramatic conflict in Rovno. But, the conflict was between a German citizen, Fritz Graebe, and the SS authorities stationed there.

Fritz Graebe was a civilian who, because of his expertise in railway construction, had been assigned by the German government to build railroads essential to the war effort in the Ukraine. Although he was a civilian, Graebe was in a position of some influence, and he used his position as a means to protect his Jewish workers and to help as many of them escape as he could. But his task was very difficult, and often dangerous as illustrated by the scene now unfolding in Rovno.

A number of Graebe's workers lived in the Rovno compound, a few miles from Sdolbonov where Graebe's offices were located. On July 11, 1942, Graebe heard rumors that there was to be a "Jewish Action" in Rovno on July 13. The action was planned by SS Major Dr. Puetz. Rovno would be Judenrein (free of Jews), a gift to Eric Koch, senior Reich commissar for the Ukraine. Acting quickly, Graebe went to Dr. Puetz. He told Puetz he had heard there might be an action in Rovno and insisted that his workers were essential to completing the railroad. Puetz denied that any such action was planned, saying that such an action would be foolish, the railways needed people, the war effort needed people. There was no reason to worry.

Graebe did not trust Puetz, and on the night of July 12 he received definite word that the action was going to take place. Quickly, Graebe went to Rovno and spent the night standing in front of the buildings where his people were housed. All night long, there was gunfire, women and children being herded into the streets and shot, houses being grenaded, large groups being gathered together to be herded to a site for mass exterminations. Word came to Graebe that seven of his men had been captured. He immediately went to where they were. With them was Dr. Puetz. Puetz spoke first.

"Why are you here, Graebe?"

"Why did you lie to me, Dr. Puetz? You told

me there would not be an action. I tell you now what I told you before. I need all my workers. I want them back, now!"

"No! I start actions, but I can't stop them. No one gets out of here alive." Puetz put his hand on his revolver.

Graebe faced him with his automatic rifle resting on his hip. Both stood motionless for several minutes, the silent standoff watched carefully by SS guards and the victims squatted on the ground. Graebe noticed Puetz place his finger into the trigger guard of his revolver and Graebe leveled his automatic at Puetz.

Suddenly, Puetz released his revolver. "Graebe! Go get the rest of your Jews, take them with you and leave."

When Graebe demanded seven of the men squatted on the ground, Puetz refused. He could get those who were not yet collected, but not those who were already there. Graebe agreed, if he pushed for the seven, he might well lose the one hundred and twenty Puetz said he could get. Graebe insisted that he be given an SS guard to protect him and his people to the edge of the compound. "The Ukrainian militiamen are drunk with killing. I want protection."

Puetz agreed, only on condition that Graebe have his people out of Rovno by 8:00 a.m. If not they would all be rounded up and brought back.

Graebe moved quickly. He went to the houses where his workers were and gave out word that they needed to meet him in the street immediately. As soon as they arrived, he organized them into columns, and then began walking at their head as he led them out of Rovno, with the SS guard in the rear. Graebe marched with the automatic weapon to his shoulder. Both Ukrainians and German SS officers let them pass. They walked slowly because most of the people were weak from hunger and fatigue. Around them were hundreds of dead bodies, and the shooting was still going on. It was a scene from hell. As they marched the dusty road to Sdolbonov, individuals hiding in the corn fields would frequently slip into their ranks.

It was night before the small exodus reached Sdolbonov where the marchers were fed and papers were issued to those who did not have them to show that they worked for Graebe. Word spread quickly. That evening, as Graebe went into town, a German officer, commented, "Here is the leader of those Jews, the Moses of Rovno."

Hindsight Questions
- What was a "Jewish Action"?
- Why did Dr. Puetz initiate a "Jewish Action" in Roveno on July 13, 1942?

Insight Questions
- What would the world be like if the thinking of men like Heinrich Himmler and Dr. Puetz prevailed?
- What is wrong with their thinking?
- What was required of Fritz Graube to save the lives of the Jews he was trying to protect?

Foresight Questions
- At the end of the day, what do you think must have gone through the mind of Fritz Graube?
- What do you think must have gone through the minds of those who had spent their day killing others?

> **Discussion Opportunity:** EPT had great hold on the minds and hearts of men like Heinrich Himmler and Dr. Puetz. Polarizer had pitted National Socialism against much of the world. Perverter befogged them with exaggerated visions of the glories of the Third Reich while at the same time judging other races of people as unworthy of sharing in that glory. To assure they wouldn't, these "subhuman" races had to be exterminated. Prevaricator somehow convinced Hitler, Himmler, Puetz and others that a beautiful, happy, culture could be built on lies, corruption, and the carcasses of their neighbors. Passionata fueled the fumes of hate and turned ordinary men into demons capable of mass murder. Fritz Graube was not taken in. He was a caring, courageous, and resourceful man who at great personal risk was determined to protect and save those people he could. Criticism helped him recognize the destructive nature of National Socialism. Creativity, Control, and Communication helped him find ways to protect the workers under his care. Character Traits: PR right, duty, ownership; SR self-denial, self-reliance; RO caring, fairness, citizenship; T honesty, dependability

ACTIVITY 71

WHO IS SHOWING RESPECT?

Present the following paired situations to your students and ask:

- Which individual/s in this situation demonstrated respect and which demonstrated disrespect?
- Why do you think (each person) acted this way?
- How would you feel if someone did (each of these things) to you?

The boys let air out of the old man's tires, then hid behind a bush to watch and see what happened. When the old man came out and saw his tires were flat, he looked very discouraged. Just then a a young man came along and seeing the problem to offered to help. Soon they had the tires pumped up and the old man was on his way.

Thelma's brother slipped into the kitchen and took the tray of brownies she had made for her sleep over. Thelma wasn't back from the movie with her friends yet, and when her mother realized what had happened she made Thelma's brother come in and help her bake a new batch of brownies.

Mort pushed Thad against the locker. "I want your lunch money and you better not tell anybody." Thad was a lot smaller than Mort, so he gave him his money. But at lunch time, Vic, seeing Thad without any lunch offered to share his with him.

Vance told the younger boys how much fun they could have smoking "grass." He even offered to give them some free. When Elliot saw what was happening he told his teacher what Vance was doing.

CHOOSING TO BE TRUSTWORTHY

Section Six

LEARNING OBJECTIVES FOR SECTION SIX

Recognize the need to be honest with ourselves

Recognize the need to be honest in relations with others

Appreciate two qualities that create trustworthiness

    Honesty

    Dependability

Desire to be trustworthy

SECTION OVERVIEW

"Trustworthy"—what a wonderful word! It means to be dependable and reliable, worthy of trust. It means to be safe, honest, and true, something to be counted on. In this section, the most important message we are communicating to youth are the many benefits of being trustworthy.

Trust is the basis of all human relations and is the foundation on which freedom rests. To the extent there is a lack of trust, there must be laws to protect us. To the extent there are laws to protect us, there is loss of freedom.

Of the great disappointments in life, none are more vexing than to have a loved one or friend violate our trust. At the same time, few things are more wearing than to have to constantly be on guard against one's associates. The great blessing of living among a law-abiding people is that we are able to live and move with some degree of safety and protection. As the proportion of people who are not law abiding increases, so also the risks and difficulties of daily living increase.

The key ingredient in trustworthiness is honesty. If we can see a thing for what it is, we can know better what to think about it and judge more accurately what to do about it. Where we get into trouble is when we trust those we ought not. Should we happen to become among those who can't be trusted by others, we become a danger to ourselves as well. To trust our own judgment and choices when others cannot is to trust that which ought not to be trusted.

Benjamin Franklin once wrote, "We can never choose evil, as evil, but under the appearance of an imaginary good." The very nature of dishonesty is that we must first practice it on ourselves before we can practice it on others. The process of altering or repressing truth so undermines human relations and so weakens the mortar of intelligent action as to render those affected by it exposed and vulnerable. Those who are unworthy of trust find themselves unable to trust others. There is no place nor any persons among whom they can be wholly safe. Required to live by their wits, they must be always on the defensive and are constantly subject to exposure and ruin.

While we may not always be able to know who else we may trust, it is essential to always be able to trust ourselves and to know that we will never willingly violate the trust of others.

ACTIVITY 72

ESSAY

This above all: to thine own self be true, And it must follow as the night the day, Thou canst not then be false to any man.

William Shakespeare

Oh, what a tangled web we weave,
When first we practice to deceive

Sir Walter Scott

1) *Assign your students to select one of the above quotes and write a one page essay addressing the question,* "What does this quote mean?"

2) *Assign your students to read a book, watch a play, TV show, or movie and write a paper exploring how either the plot or characters in the story exemplified one or both of the above quotes.*

Hindsight Questions
- What did you learn from this activity?

Insight Questions
- Why is it important to understand the meaning of these quotes?

Foresight Questions
- How might you use these quotes as a guide for choices you make?

ACTIVITY 73

TRUSTWORTHINESS IS. . . .

ADVANCE PREPARATION : *Photocopy the activity sheet on page 153 for each student. Have students complete the activity sheet*

Hindsight Questions
- How difficult was it to complete this activity sheet?

Insight Questions
- * What do words like stable, wobbly, secure, dirty, slippery, etc. have to do with choices people make?
- What do they have to do with trust?

Foresight Questions
- Which of these words would you like to describe you?

TRUSTWORTHINESS IS. . . .

Separate each word in the list below by putting a / mark in between each word. After you have identified all the words, write each word in one of the columns below under the heading you think it belongs.

```
S T A B L E S O L I D B R O K E N S T R O
N G W O B B L Y F I R M W E A K E N H E A
L T H Y H O N E S T T R U E L O O S E S A
F E S L I P P E R Y S I C K D E C A Y E D
S E C U R E F R A Y E D T R U S T Y D I R
T Y D A M A G E D D E F E C T I V E W H O
L E D E C E I V E F A L S E S E L F I S H
```

TRUSTWORTHY   UNTRUSTWORTHY

_____   _____

_____   _____

_____   _____

_____   _____

_____   _____

_____   _____

_____   _____

_____   _____

_____   _____

_____   _____

ACTIVITY 74

POOR PETER PIPER

ADVANCE PREPARATION: *Photocopy the stories on page 155 for student use.*

Individually or in small groups have your students read the Peter Piper stories, one at a time. For fun, invite students to read selected stories out loud as fast as they can to the rest of the class. Invite other class members to read along. Have competitions as to who can read the stories fastest without getting tounge-tied. Then discuss the associated questions.

74-1   Penelope Palmer Cheats Peter Piper

Ask and discuss:
- What is important to Penelope?
- Which EPT agents is Penelope listening to?
- Which C skills is Peter missing?

74-2   Patty Potter's Prevarication

Ask and discuss:
- How did Patty fail to live up to the trust that was placed in her?
- By telling her Poppa a lie, how did Patty make the situation worse?
- What is the difference between breaking a promise and telling a lie?

74-3   Peter Purloins Paula's Pie

Ask and discuss:
- Which C skills could help Peter find a happier solution?
- How did Peter demonstrate a lack of respect for others?
- Why is it hard to trust people who lack self-control or respect for others?

Discussion Opportunity: There is no safety in company with those who are dishonest. If a person will lie cheat or steal for personal gain, anyone who associates with them is at risk. Moreover, such people are a risk to themselves. Since no one can trust them, they can trust no one. Yet, no one is smart enough and clever enough at all times to be certain of avoiding either getting caught by their enemies or cheated by their friends. Character Traits: RO caring, fairness, citizenship; T honesty, dependability

---

Penelope Palmer Cheats Peter Piper

Peter Piper was poor. Peter's profession was picking pickled peppers. Eating pickled peppers was not a particularly popular pastime, (just think how pleasing pickled peppers are to your palate) and pickled pepper pickers were pretty poorly paid. To make things worse, Peter's employer was Penelope Palmer, a pitifully penurious piker who wouldn't flinch an inch to pinch a pound, much less a penny from poor people like Peter.

Part of the problem was that Peter was poorly prepared for plunderers like Penelope. He couldn't add or subtract. So Penelope pinched a penny per peck from every peck of pickled peppers Peter picked. Instead of the four pence per peck Penelope promised to pay Peter, Penelope only paid Peter three pence per peck. Peter was poor and would probably be perpetually poor as long as he picked pickled peppers for the penny pinching Penelope Palmer.

Retell the story (using as many "P" words as you can) to make Penelope a more honest person.

Patty Potter's Prevarication

Peter Piper was a penniless peasant. Picking pickled peppers was not a particularly popular profession and only the poorest of peasants picked pickle peppers. Despite his poverty, Peter Piper was a pleasant peasant, and was pals with Patty Potter's Poppa. Peter Piper was feeling pretty poorly so Poppa Potter promised to have his daughter Patty bring Peter a pot of potato porridge. Patty Potter made particularly palatable potato porridge and Poppa Potter asked Patty to prepare a pot of hot potato porridge to take to Peter. Patty promised Poppa she would prepare the potato porridge for Peter.

Patty put to, picking, peeling, and preparing potatoes to make a porridge of prodigious proportions. But, just when Patty had her porridge prepared, Paula Puckett invited Patty to a party and asked her to bring some of her particularly palatable potato porridge. So Patty took her porridge to Paula's party instead of taking it to poor Peter who was perilously close to perishing for want of provender.

The next day, Poppa Potter went to visit Peter Piper and found poor Peter in a pitiful plight. Poppa Potter pitied the poor peasants perilous position and was pretty peeved Patty had not provided Peter the potato porridge he had promised. When Poppa Potter asked Patty why she had not provided the promised potato porridge to Peter, Patty pretended to pout and then performed a pernicious perfidy by proclaiming that her potato porridge had been poached by a pair of ponderous plunderers.

Retell the story (using as many "P" words as you can) to make Patty more trustworthy.

Peter Purloins Paula's Pie

Paula Puckett prepared a pot of potato porridge and a purple plum pie for her Poppa. Poppa Puckett was particularly partial to peas and parsnips with purple plum pie, but alas, Paula had no parsnips and peas. However, nothing pleased Poppa Puckett's palate more then purple plum pie. Paula put the pie on the porch to cool, and it's pungent aroma permeated the air.

Just then, Peter Piper, after a day of picking pickled peppers passed by pleasantly pondering a plate of peas and parsnips from the pot he kept perpetually prepared at his place.

Unfortunately, Peter had a purple passion for plum pie and like Poppa Puckett had a particular fondness for peas and parsnips with his pie. As the pungent oder of Paula's pie penetrated Peter's senses, Peter abandoned both prudence and principle and purloined Paula's pie from the Puckett's porch. As a result, Poppa and Paula Puckett had to be content with potato porridge while Peter Piper pigged out on parsnips and peas with purple plum pie.

Retell the story (using as many "P" words as you can) to give a happier ending to the story.

ACTIVITY 75

EDISON'S DEMONSTRATION

Several men were gathered around Thomas Edison as he gave them their final instructions. "The representatives from Baltimore will be arriving shortly." said Edison in conclusion. "I need not tell you how important this demonstration is. Unless we convince large cities of the benefits of installing electrical lighting systems, the only place where electric lights will ever be seen is right here in Menlo Park. Now, you remember that when we had the aldermen from New York city here a few weeks ago, someone tried to sabotage our demonstration by short-circuiting the electrical current. Although only three lights went out, it caused a disruption and raised questions about reliability. We must be on the guard for another similar attempt tonight. Only this time we want to catch the culprit. As you circulate among the guests, I want you to be on the alert for anyone who may attempt to interfere with the wires. Now, keep a sharp eye, and let me know if any thing unusual happens."

As the men dispersed to their designated posts, Edison surveyed the scene before him. It was indeed impressive. Hundreds of light globes, strung through the leafless trees, magnificently illuminated Menlo Park. It had been arranged that the party should arrive after dark. "Surely, they cannot help but be impressed." thought Edison to himself as he watched his staff moving about the trees and buildings as clearly as if it were day.

The Baltimore committee arrived within the hour. As they stepped from their coaches, it was evident they were impressed. The evening progressed well, with Edison and his staff busily answering questions and explaining how the system worked. Edison was visiting with several individuals when suddenly several lights went out and a cry arose from across the yard. There was a great deal of commotion, but Edison could not see what was happening. Presently two of his men, firmly holding a man between them, made their way to where Edison was.

"Lookey what we found sir! This gentleman is responsible for the lights that just went out."

With that they, pulled from the sleeve of his coat, a long piece of number 10 wire which he had run up one sleeve of his coat, across his shoulders and down the other sleeve. "What do you suppose he was doing with this, sir?" the men asked. "I can easily guess." said Edison, "What I want to know is why?"

"I think I can tell you," spoke up one of the guests standing by, "this man has a large interest in the Baltimore Gas Company. Those people must be very worried about what you are doing here."

"That explains a lot." Edison replied. "But perhaps this good man has really done us a favor. You will notice that even with a deliberate attempt to sabotage the system, only four lights went out. Several hundred are still lit and were unaffected. This is because there are copper wire fuses installed throughout the system to keep large numbers of lights from going out because of local shorts in the wiring."

Discussion Opportunity: Thomas Edison was a man who had highly developed C skills. So when Prevaricator convinced the investor from the Baltimore Gas Company to sabotage the lighting system, Edison was ready for him. In addition to having his men on the lookout for someone attempting to cause problems, Edison had installed copper fuses to prevent any wide scale blackout. Had this man not given in to EPT, and had used the skills of Criticism and Creativity more effectively, he would have recognized the future was bright for both electric and gas energy and perhaps might have chosen to invest in electricity rather than attempt to sabotage it. Character Traits: PR ownership; RO citizenship; T honesty, dependability

 The Seven C's of Thinking Clearly Grades 5-9, Copyright 2003, George L. Rogers. Reproducible by owner for classroom use only.

ACTIVITY 76

THE HOUSE OF SHAWS

Adapted from Robert Louis Stevenson's novel *Kidnapped*

David listened intently as Mr. Rankeillor spoke. "But your uncle, Mr. David, was not always old, and what may perhaps surprise you more, not always ugly. He had a fine gallant air; people stood in their doors to look after him, as he went by upon a mettle horse. I have seen it with these eyes, and I confess, not without envy; for I was a plain lad myself, and a plain man's son. . ."

David was indeed surprised. To imagine his uncle Ebeneezer; a shriveled, bent old man who lived alone in the elegant squalor of a run down mansion known as the House of Shaws; to think of this miserly, cruel old man with few friends, hated by his tenants, and viewed with dislike and distrust by his neighbors, as a gallant, handsome young man was almost too much.

Mr. Rankeillor continued, "You will be wondering, no doubt, about your father and your uncle? To be sure, it is a singular tale; and the explanation is one that I blush to tell you. For, the matter hinges on a love affair. The two lads fell in love, and that with the same lady, your mother.

Mr. Ebenezer, who was the admired, the beloved, and the spoiled one, was, no doubt, mighty certain of the victory; and when he found that he had deceived himself, he screamed like a peacock. The whole country heard of it; now he lay sick at home, with his silly family standing around the bed in tears; now he rode from public-house to public-house and shouted his sorrows into the lug of Tom, Dick, and Harry.

Your father, Mr. David, was a kind gentleman; but was dolefully weak. He took all this folly with a long countenance; and one day—by your leave!—resigned the lady. She was no such fool, however; it's from her you must inherit your excellent good sense; and she refused to be bandied from one to another. Both got upon their knees to her; and the upshot of the matter for that while,

was that she showed them both the door. The end of the matter, however, was that from one height to another of squalling and sentimental selfishness by your uncle, and from one concession to another by your father, they came at last to a sort of bargain, from whose ill-results you have recently been smarting. Your father took the lady, your uncle the estate.

This piece of foolishness upon your father's part, as it was unjust in itself, has brought forth a monstrous family of injustices. Your father and mother lived and died poor folk; you were poorly reared; and in the mean while, what a time it has been for the poor tenants on the estate of Shaws! And I might add, what a time for Mr. Ebenezer!"

David replied, "That is the strangest part of all, that a man's nature should thus change."

"True," said Mr. Rankeillor. "And yet I imagine it was natural enough. Ebenezer could not think that he had played a handsome part. Those who knew the story gave him the cold shoulder, those who knew it not, having seen one brother disappear, and the other succeed in the estate, raised a cry of murder; so that upon all sides, Ebenezer found himself without friends. Money was all he got by his bargain; and money came to be all he cared about. He was selfish when he was young, he is selfish now that he is old; and the latter end of his selfishness you have seen for yourself."

With this last statement, David's mind flashed back to his recent experiences with his uncle Ebenezer. Now he understood, why his uncle had been so fearful of him. With a mixture of pity and anger he reflected upon the evening when his uncle had tried to send him to his death by asking him climb the unfinished staircase in the dark. If it had not been for his own caution and a flash of lightening which revealed his danger to him, he would surely not be here talking to Mr. Rankeillor now. Similarly fate had favored his escape from the clutches of Captain Hoseason who, at his uncle's instructions, had kidnapped him.

Through David's mind quickly passed the scene in the ship's round house when he and Alan Breck had fought off Hoseason and his crew as they tried to kill Alan in an attempt to steal the belt of gold he was wearing. In the end, most of the captain's crew were either killed or wounded. David thought about the next eighteen months he was to spend with Alan in the highlands of Scotland, wandering with lawless people, making his bed upon the hills and under the sky, frequently ill, often in danger, and barely escaping one breathtaking adventure after another.

Yes, David Balfour, could observe the effects of his uncle's greed and selfishness with an insight he could never have imagined when he first arrived in Edinburgh a few months ago. He had suffered much, but he couldn't help wonder if his uncle's suffering, in the end, was not the greatest suffering of all. Without family or friends, and continually troubled by bouts of shame, fear, and envy, his uncle Ebenezer had probably never experienced a truly happy day for many, many years.

Hindsight Questions
- What was the bargain struck between David's father and his uncle?
- What did David's uncle do to David?

Insight Questions
- Why was David's uncle not a trustworthy man?
- What caused him to become this why?

Foresight Questions
- What benefit did Ebeneeser receive from his wealth?
- What are frequent consequences of selfish and dishonest choices?

Discussion Opportunity: Possessit gained a great hold on David's uncle as a young man. Perverter aided Possessit by exaggerating the importance of the things Ebeneeser wanted and the benefit he would gain by having them. Perverter also minimized in David's father's mind the need he would have for his share of the estate. Prevaricator became Ebeneeser's aid in attempting to get rid of David. But it didn't work. Relying on Control with some help from Creativity, Concentration, and Alan Breck, David was able to escape Captain Hoseason. In the end, Captain Hoseason, who also had fallen victim to Possessit and Perverter, was poorly paid for his greed. All in all, it cost the captain his ship and most of his crew. Character Traits: PR ownership; RO caring, fairness; T honesty, dependability.

ACTIVITY 77

A TRILOGY IN SELF-DECEIT

Read the following poems and discuss the associated questions.

77-1   Erica Monica Louisa McKeever

Erica Monica Louisa McKeever
Practiced the art of self-deceiver.
With hardly a thought and nary a think,
She could lie to herself as quick as a wink.

"I didn't do it." to her mother she said,
Hardly aware of the other thought in her head.
"No one will know if never I tell,
And if they don't know, it'll be just as well."

What is Erica missing? What is she without?
What is her problem all about?
If you can tell me, I'd like you to now,
Please give me the whatfor, the whyfor, and how.

Ask and discuss:
- In what way is Erica deceiving herself?
- Is it true no one will ever know?
- How might Erica's lie undermine her mother's trust in her?
- Which C skills can help Erica in this situation?

77-2   Gustollen Guthiever

Now the greatest of crooks, Gustollen Guthiever,
Was also an accomplished self-deceiver.
In stealing from others, he thought only of gain,
And never considered the probable pain.

"It's quick and it's easy, not very hard work.
And I'll do very well," he thought with a smirk.
"I'll live life in luxury, much like a King.
And not have to worry, not over a thing."

What has swollen Gustollen's poor brain?
To think something stolen is ever true gain?
If you can tell me, I'd like you to now,
Please give me the whatfor, the whyfor, and how.

Ask and discuss:
- In what way is Gustollen deceiving himself?
- What might Gustollen have to worry about?
- How is Gustollen's stealing hurtful to himself and to others?
- Which C skills can help Gustollen?

77-3   Martin Maloney Baloney Bo Peep

Now Martin Maloney Baloney Bo Peep
Was so accomplished in self-deceit.
That he was willing to cheat on a test,
To prove to others he was really the best.

"If I get the best score." was thought that he had,
"I'll be top in the class and my dad'll be glad.
Cause getting an A is a lot better than B,
And a whole lot better than a lousy old C."

Why is Martin Maloney Baloney Bo Peep
So highly successful at self-deceit?
If you can tell me, I'd like you to now,
Please give me the whatfor, the whyfor, and how.

Ask and discuss:
- In what way is Martin deceiving himself?
- Will Martin really be best?
- Will Martin's dad really be glad?
- How is Martin's cheating hurtful to himself and to others?
- Which C skills can help Martin?

BIOGRAPHY

ACTIVITY 78

TRIAL OF THE JOAN OF ARC

For nearly a hundred years, France had been ruled by England. And for nearly a hundred years, the French had been scorned by the English. A favorite joke among the English soldiers was that they did not know what a Frenchman looked like because every time they went to battle all they could see was their backs. French pride, French self-respect was nearly extinguished. Only a small glow remained, like the last smoldering embers of a fire about to go out. That is until a small, slender, seventeen year old girl stepped forward and boldly declared to the King of France that she had been called of God to lead the French army to victory against the English and to drive them out of France.

In less than six months, Joan, "with the sure and clear judgment of a trained general of twenty or thirty year's experience." had led her armies to battle, had broken the siege of Orleans and won several other major victories. The very mention of Joan of Arc struck fear into the heart of every English soldier and inspired confidence in the heart of every French patriot. France was on its way to becoming free. But, such was not to be, at least not at the time. Joan was captured in a skirmish by the Duke of Burgandy, and put up for ransom. But it was not the King of France who paid her ransom, but rather a French Bishop, the infamous Pierre Cauchon of Beauvals.

Though French by birth, Cauchon was in fact an English vassal. The English had seen their opportunity and now was the time to act. English power could kill the body of Joan of Arc, but could not quench the flame of patriotism her very name inspired. No, a much more subtle scheme was needed to rid themselves of this dreaded opponent. If the church could be used to disgrace her name and to destroy her influence on the hearts of her fellow countrymen, English supremacy could again be reinstated. All that was

needed was to convince the French people that Joan of Arc was acting under the influence of devils rather than the inspiration of heaven. No one doubted that she had heard voices and that they had guided her in leading her armies in victory. To show, by whatever means, that these voices were of the devil and that Joan was a heretic, an apostate to the Christian faith, would seal her death and forever disgrace her name.

Cauchon was just the man for a job like this. Motivated by greed and ambition, devoid of respect for the laws of either God or man, and possessed of a clever and cunning mind, there was nothing Cauchon would not do to advance his own self-interest. His job was to try Joan before a church court and to prove that she was a devil worshiper.

Rouen was selected to be the site of the great trial. There the young maiden was placed in chains in a dark dungeon and Cauchon began his work. For more than two months Cauchon prepared his evidence, picking anything that might be injurious to Joan and suppressing anything that might be favorable. He packed his court with some fifty learned clerics, French in name but English in sympathy. These were to be her inquisitors.

Yet Joan, for her part, was to be allowed no witnesses, no counsel, no help of any kind in preparing her defense. This unlearned, untutored girl was to be confronted by fifty of the most learned and best trained clerics in France, all of whom had in mind the outcome even before the trial. It was thought it would be a quick and easy job to convict Joan of heresy and put her to death.

But such was not to be the case. Joan had been captured, but not conquered. Her defense was simple, clear spoken statements of truth. At first Cauchon had hired clerks to make a special report in which the meaning of Joan's answers were to be garbled and twisted, and then to pass them on to the crowds gathered outside the fortress in which the trial was being held. But when the clerks heard Joan's answers and realized what they were being asked to do, they revolted and made a straight report. This infuriated Cauchon. The clerks were threatened with death and sent away. Instead of days, the trial went on for weeks. Day after day, sitting alone on a small bench, dressed in black male garb, Joan answered the questions of her fifty accusers. Yet, they could find nothing in her worthy of death, and as time wore on, many were becoming sympathetic to Joan.

Cauchon changed his tactics. He dismissed most of the court, and retained only a few clerics who were solidly in the English pocket. The trial was now held in secret and barred to the public. The outcome was the production of a paper containing an admission by Joan that she was guilty of twelve sins against against the church, all of which were based on lies. One clause stated that she had threatened with death any who would not obey her. Not true. Another said she claimed that she had never committed any sin. Again, not true. A third, although Joan had high church authority for the wearing of male dress in battle, stated that Joan had sinned in wearing male clothing, and that, as a condition of repentance, she would never again wear male dress. It was this last clause which was to lead to her death.

Because Joan could not read, Cauchon was able to trick her into signing the above confession. Cauchon first read to Joan a paper in which it was agreed that she would wear women's clothing if the trial would be moved to another tribunal. Joan agreed because she felt she might get a more fair hearing in another setting. Instead however, Cauchon placed before her the confession statement to sign. That night, while asleep in her dungeon cell, all of Joan's clothing was stolen except for one set of of male dress. The next day, when she was discovered dressed again in men's clothing, it was given out as proof that Joan of Arc was an incorrigible, unrepentant heretic, worthy of death.

Joan was sentenced to die by fire at the stake. She accepted her fate with courage and serenity. But as she had prophesied during the trial, within twenty years France was again free from English dominion. In time the true facts of her trial came to light, and the verdict of the court was over turned. Joan was vindicated, and her life has become a symbol of faith, courage, and virtue to people everywhere.

Hindsight Questions
- What motivated Cauchon to deceive Joan and others concerned with her trial?
- What C skill did Joan lack that enabled him to succeed?

Insight Questions
- Why are people who lack C skills vulnerable to the agents of EPT?
- Which C skills did Joan seem to have in abundance?
- Why are all of the C skills necessary?

Foresight Questions
- What can you learn from the trial of the Joan of Arc?

Discussion Opportunity: Possessit possessed Gauchon. His desires for wealth and position made him willing to do anything necessary to put Joan away. Prevaricator gave him the tools needed to deceive any one deficient in the C skills. As a result he gained his end. Whether he gained any great benefit during his life is up for question. But, the reality is that truth and goodness suffer when they do not have sufficient defenders who possess the C skills. So also do individuals who are governed by leaders who have sold themselves to EPT. Character Traits: RO caring, fairness, citizenship; T honesty

---

ACTIVITY 79

HEAVY DUTY DILEMMAS

ADVANCE PREPARATION: *Photocopy page 164 and cut out each dilemma.*

Divide class into small groups and give each a dilemma. Have them discuss the situation, and consider their answers to the respective questions. Allow about ten minutes and then have a spokesman for each group read the dilemma to the class and present their answers to the questions.

Hindsight Questions
- Why are these situations considered heavy duty?

Insight Questions
- What do these situations all have in common?
- Why must each person in each situation make his or her own choice?

Foresight Questions
- What are some ways in which these individuals may be held accountable for the choices they make?
- Although, in most cases several people were involved, why is each person individually accountable?

Discussion Opportunity: Life sometimes presents us with tough choices. It often requires courage and vision to make the right choice. But many choices we have to live with for a long time and it is important to get them right. Those who make choices contrary to their conscience are on shaky ground. In allowing external influences to control our choices we we often do things we later regret. When people are engaged in activities that are hurtful to others, there are far reaching effects. The nature of injuring others is to create enemies. Another natural consequence is the loss of self-respect and peace of mind. Still another is the loss of the ability to think clearly for, to justify such actions, one has to draw on support from EPT. Character Traits: SR self-understanding, self-denial; RO caring, fairness, citizenship; T honesty, dependability

---

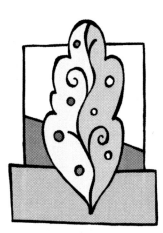

Heavy Duty Dilemmas

Jamal had to make a decision. His buddies expected him to be with them when they took down the Gonzales girl for ratting on them. They had it planned to gang rape her when she came home that night. If he wasn't with them, they could easily turn on him. The rule was that everyone had to be there and participate, but....

- What are Jamal's choices?
- Why is this an important choice for Jamal?
- Which C skills and Character traits will help Jamal in this situation?
- What might be the consequences of Jamal's choices now? Five years from now?

Terri paced the floor. Tonight was the big party. All her friends would be there. She knew the plans. Crystal's parents were out of town. The boy's were to get there about nine. They were bringing the booze. John said that they would even have some cocaine with them. It was to be a big blast, but.....
- What are Terri's choices?
- Why is this an important choice for Terri?
- Which C skills and Character traits will help Terri in this situation?
- What might be the consequences of Terri's choices now and in the future?

Tony had never done it, but the idea excited him. He liked to watch big fires burn. He even felt he had a reason. He had been fired from his job the day before, and wanted to get even. What better way. But......
- What are Tony's choices?
- Why is this an important choice for Tony?
- What C skills and character traits can Tony use to guide him?
- What might be the consequences of Tony's choices now and in the future?

The boys had been talking. The more they talked the more heated the conversation became. They didn't like the idea that a new family had moved into the block. The family couldn't speak English and belonged to an oriental religion of some sort. They wanted to show them they weren't welcome. Someone suggested they throw some rocks through their windows. The idea caught hold and they began to move toward the house. Bix was moving with them, but......
- What are Bix's choices?
- Why is this an important choice for Bix?
- What C skills and character traits can Bix use to guide him?
- What might be the consequences of Bix's choices now and in the future?

The girls were going shopping at the mall. Beth suggested an idea. "Let's see how much stuff we can get without paying for it. We'll go in pairs, one is to act as a look out while the other takes the item they want. Just wear a big coat to hid things under." All the girls thought this was a great idea. But Amy.....
- What are Amy's choices?
- Why is this an important choice for Amy?
- What C skills and character traits can Amy use to guide her?
- What might be the consequences of Amy's choices now and in the future?

Rhetta wasn't like them. She had some kind of disease that affected her body so she couldn't walk right. Laughing at her when she walked by had gotten to be the thing to do. It did look sort of funny to watch her walk. Edy was often in the group when this happened, but....
- What are Edy's choices?
- Why are these moral choices?
- What C skills and character traits can Edy use to guide her?
- What might be the consequences of Edy's choices now and in the future?

INDEX SECTION

Index

Character Trait Cross Reference Guide

All the activities and stories in The Seven C's of thinking Clearly for Grade levels 2-6, provide opportunities to discuss various character traits. Some activities provide opportunities to discuss several character traits. The following cross-reference guide indicates the character traits each activity or story best illustrates. Character traits in the book are categorized as follows:

- **Personal Responsibility** encompasses the right to act, the duty to act, ownership of choices and actions, and accountability for actions.
- **Self-Respect** includes discussion of Self-Understanding, Self-Denial, Self-Reliance which includes Initiative, Industriousness, Persistence, Patience, and Resourcefulness.
- **Respect for Others** provides discussion opportunities for Caring, Fairness, and Citizenship which includes honoring rightful authority, and honoring the rights and property of others.
- **Trustworthiness** incorporates honesty and dependability.

PERSONAL RESPONSIBILITY

RIGHT TO ACT
The Martyrdom of Andy Drake, 34
What's In a Name?, 36
Discrimination Activity, 39
We Hold These Truths to Be Self-Evident, 61
The Case of the Missing Stradivarius, 63
I Struggled to Stay Awake, 65 slf rel
Among My Detractors, 66
The Beginnings of a Noble Prize, 68
Frederick Douglass Learns to Read and Write , 70
But You Forgot the Candlesticks, 82
Al and Irene, 94
The Last of the Human Freedoms, 96
I Plead Guilty to All the Charges, 101
Korczak's Orphans, 112

Return From Ravensbruk, 130
Harriet Begins Uncle Tom's Cabin, 136
Lunatics Don't Feel the Cold, 138
July 13, 140
Trial of the Joan of Arc, 155
Heavy Duty Dilemmas , 163

DUTY TO ACT
Beware of Error-Prone Thinking, 4
Brain Food for Error-Prone Thinking, 12
Self-Talk, 13
EPT Agents at Work , 15
What Does it Cost?, 18
How Much Land Does a Man Need, 21
So Convenient to Be a Reasonable Creature, 24
What About Ryan?, 27

Those Who Believe in Invisible Thread, 31
What's In a Name?, 36
Discrimination Activity, 39
The Nature of Things, 40
Quoth the Philosopher, 42
The Great Debate, 54
911 For the CT Team, 55
Benjamin Franklin Uses the Seven C Skills, 58
The Case of the Missing Stradivarius, 63
Washington's Maxims, 88
The Chicken and the Eagle, 90
TFAC Connection, 101
There Are Really Wolves, 99
I Plead Guilty to All the Charges, 101
The Real Hardship of This Place, 110
Korczak's Orphans, 112

GREAT LESSONS FROM GREAT LIVES

Book One Grades 2-6

Book Two Grades 5-9